Australian Curriculum

ENGLISH
YEAR
9

A student workbook

Leanne Bondin & Adam Kealley

insight
▸innovative ▸engaging ▸evolving

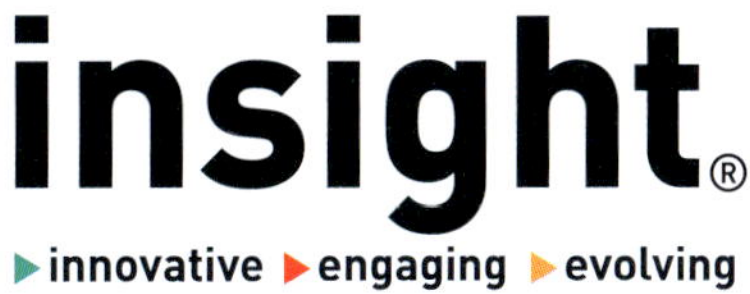

First published in 2023

Insight Publications Pty Ltd

3/350 Charman Road

Cheltenham Victoria 3192

Australia

Tel: +61 3 8571 4950

Fax: +61 3 8571 0257

Email: books@insightpublications.com.au

www.insightpublications.com.au

A catalogue record for this book is available from the National Library of Australia

Australian Curriculum English Year 9 / Leanne Bondin and Adam Kealley

ISBN: 9781922771704

Edited by Lisa Neale

Proofread by Penny Mansley

Cover and Internal design by Melisa Paredes

Typsetting by Kobie van Jaarsveld

Printed by Markono Print Media Pte Ltd

Contents

Note to teachers

The *Australian Curriculum English* series is designed to assist student development of English skills, knowledge and understanding in interesting, engaging ways. The series aligns with Version 9.0 of the Australian Curriculum, ensuring that the Literature, Language and Literacy strands of the curriculum, as well as their sub-strands and threads, are seamlessly integrated and well balanced across the units of work. Each text in the series covers the entire curriculum content for its corresponding year level at least once, and in most instances several times, in order to highlight the varied approaches available to teachers and their students. Relevant Australian Curriculum content is specified in the introduction to each unit.

Each *Australian Curriculum English* book comprises 12 units, each of which is centred on a unifying theme, text type or significant English skill. Cumulatively, the units provide ample opportunity for students to practise their writing, reading, listening, speaking and viewing skills. The units can be completed in any order; teachers may find it useful to dip in and out of units in ways that complement their established teaching and learning programs.

The units include a number of text extracts, from familiar 'classics' to more contemporary and original texts. The extracts have been selected for their potential to illustrate particular curriculum content in action; teachers are encouraged to examine the texts independently to assess their suitability for their specific school context or cohort. While each unit includes multiple activities related to the unit focus, the final two units in the book closely target the specific comprehension strategies and grammar, punctuation and word knowledge specified in the Australian Curriculum English 7–10.

A range of colour-coded '**Check for understanding**' and '**Reflecting and discussing**' activities are embedded within the content of units 1–10. These activities are designed to:

- help students strengthen and deepen their understanding of the concepts covered
- encourage students to reflect carefully upon the content in relation to their own lives and experiences
- facilitate meaningful whole-class or small-group interactions and discussion around the content.

Several '**Get creative**' activities within units 1–10 prompt students to create their own texts in a range of forms by practising writing, speaking and creating for different audiences and purposes. All activities make ideal classroom and/or homework tasks. Many of the written activities included can be completed within the fill-in lines provided.

As English teachers ourselves, we appreciate the importance of practical and helpful resources that supplement our own classroom practices and assist students to master essential curriculum content and skills. We sincerely hope that this series does just that for you and your students. To access suggested solutions to the activities in this workbook, please email us at: sales@insightpublications.com.au

Flash fiction

Have you ever found it difficult to concentrate for long enough to read a whole novel or even a short story? Does your mind wander or get distracted by other things you need to do? Do you like stories that are exciting and engaging? Flash fiction might be the answer! Flash fiction features a few characters at most and a very condensed plot that engages readers quickly. This unit will help you to understand the origins and features of flash fiction, to appreciate some examples of this type of writing and to craft your own works of flash fiction.

In this unit you will learn:

- how authors adapt text structures and language features to produce very short written texts
- how authors vary sentence structures and organise ideas to shape meaning
- to create and edit your own flash fiction.

Curriculum content

Australian Curriculum content description	Content code
Examine how authors adapt and subvert text structures and language features by experimenting with spoken, written, visual and multimodal elements, and their combination.	AC9E9LA03
Identify how authors vary sentence structures creatively for effects, such as intentionally using a dependent clause on its own or a sentence fragment.	AC9E9LA05
Create and edit literary texts, that may be a hybrid, that experiment with text structures, language features and literary devices for purposes and audiences.	AC9E9LE06
Analyse the organisation of ideas in paragraphs and extended texts, and evaluate its impact on meaning.	AC9E9LY04

Origins and types of flash fiction

'Flash fiction' is the name for a category of stories under about 1000 words in length, although they can be even shorter than this. Flash fiction is sometimes called 'short shorts', 'microfiction', 'sudden fiction' or 'nanofiction', depending on its length. The form originated many centuries ago in Ancient Rome. Although flash fiction is characterised by its short length, writing of this kind still offers a complete story rather than just a fragment.

1.1

Check for understanding

Find definitions for the following types of flash fiction. If conducting an online search for definitions, make sure you add the word 'fiction' to your search terms.

Types of flash fiction	Definitions
twitterature	
hint fiction	
drabble	
dribble	
postcard fiction	

Features of flash fiction

The features of flash fiction are similar to those of any fictional **narrative**. They often contain the same narrative **conventions** as short stories and novels, such as characters, settings and plots. These elements combine to convey ideas and **themes**, which may be just as important as ideas or messages in other, longer texts that you have read or viewed. Good flash fiction writers also create a distinctive atmosphere or mood in their stories.

narrative The selection and sequencing of events or experiences, real or imagined, to tell a story to entertain, engage, inform and extend imagination, typically using an orientation, complication and resolution
convention An accepted practice that has developed over time and is generally used and understood (e.g. use of punctuation)
theme The main idea, concept or message of a text

What makes flash fiction unique is that it develops these elements in very condensed and compressed ways. There is generally only one main idea or plot thread in a work of flash fiction. Characters and settings are also usually very limited in number. The common features of flash fiction are detailed in the following table. Look out for them in the flash fiction piece beneath the table.

Features	Definitions	Examples
narrative structure	the way that plot is organised and unfolds; could be linear, chronological etc.	
narrative point of view	the position from which the story is told; might be first or third person, omniscient or restricted etc.	
characterisation	the way a writer crafts details of a character, such as their actions, dialogue or appearance	
conflict	a literary element that adds tension and uncertainty to the plot by working as a challenge or obstacle to the character/s	
setting	the world created within the text, including where and when the plot takes place	
imagery	visually descriptive or figurative language used to represent things that appeal to the senses of the reader	

She's Gone

I aim for the lips but she turns her head. Some of my spit sticks to her cheek.

Her eyes find the ground without pausing at my hundred-push-up-a-day-chest.

I know it's over.

'Why?' I say.

She shrugs.

'Tell me.'

She turns away.

I grab a smooth shoulder and spin her; our noses collide. She smells like peppermint.

'Tell me', I say. 'Please?'

The muscles in her face form a smile, but she's not smiling. She rubs her teeth. 'You used to taste sweet,' she says.

'Now ...'

She's walking away.

I yell. 'You're just ... bracist!'

She's gone.

Pat Flynn

1.2

Check for understanding

1 Read the flash fiction story 'She's Gone' and complete the right-hand column of the table before the story using examples from the story.

2 The story is only 95 words long. Do you think it can be considered a complete story? Give reasons for your answer.

___

___

___

3 What do you think is the theme or main idea of the story?

___

___

Text structure

Flash fiction often adapts the traditional story structure which contains an orientation (or exposition), rising action, climax, falling action and resolution. A condensed approach is used by flash fiction writers because they need to move the story along very quickly. They often reduce the story into a shorter three-part structure such as the one that Katherine Batchelor (2012) outlines below.

Conflict (opening hook) → Crisis (turning point) → Connect-the-dot (resolution)

This compressed flash fiction text structure is an adaptation of the regular 'exposition/ orientation – rising action – climax – falling action – resolution' phases of a narrative.

1.3

Check for understanding

1 Circle which of the following options could be considered the 'conflict' phase of 'She's Gone' – that is, the part that works as a hook to engage the reader.

the noses colliding   the failed kiss   the narrator yelling

2 Circle which of the following options could be considered the 'crisis' or turning point of 'She's Gone', where the tension is most heightened.

the girl's rejection of the narrator   the girl's shrug   the girl walking away

3 What realisation could be considered the 'connect-the-dot' resolution of 'She's Gone', where the reader has to fill in the gaps to make sense about missing parts of the plot? What inference do we make at the end of the story about why the girl is no longer interested in the narrator?

____

____

Multiple meanings

It is important to understand that even though flash fiction might be short, its ideas and themes can be just as compelling, complex and intellectual as those of any other story. In fact, the appeal of flash fiction is its ability to generate profound meaning in so few words. Readers often have to fill in the gaps formed by what is *not* said in the story, which can lead to many different readings or interpretations of the text's meaning.

A famous six-word example of flash fiction, attributed to Ernest Hemingway, is reproduced below.

> For sale: baby shoes, never worn.

Even though the flash fiction story above is only six words long, it generates many possible questions and answers, or 'meanings', in the minds of readers. There is no single correct interpretation of what the story means. Readers can fill in the gaps left by the information *not* included in the story and develop their own interpretation or understanding of it.

1.4 Reflecting and discussing

Discuss the following questions in pairs, in small groups or with the whole class as directed by your teacher.

1 Why do you think the baby shoes were never worn?

2 Why are the baby shoes being sold?

3 Who is selling the baby shoes?

4 What mood is evoked by the story?

1.5 Get creative

Create three of your own six-word short stories about something that is 'for sale'.

____

____

____

Organisation of ideas and impact on meaning

Flash fiction relies on the clever, economical use of words. This means that the author has to be very selective in the way they use words because they don't have many at their disposal. They need to choose words carefully and combine them in sentences creatively to produce effects, such as contributing to the meaning or **tone** of a story.

Sentence structures affect the organisation of ideas and shape the meaning created in texts. Here are some examples of how sentence structures can do this.

» A sentence fragment lacks a **verb** or **subject**, so while it is usually considered a grammatical error, it can be used to create an interesting effect by adding emphasis or creating atmosphere in creative writing like flash fiction.

» Repetition of the same combination of words or types of words across consecutive sentences can create rhythm or add impact.

» Variation of sentence length can enhance reader interest and engagement.

tone The mood created by the language features used by an author and the way the text makes the reader feel
verb A word class that expresses processes that include doing, feeling, thinking, saying and relating
subject A word or group of words (usually a noun group/phrase) in a sentence or clause representing the person, thing or idea doing the action that follows (e.g. 'The dog [subject] was barking')

Read the following work of flash fiction, paying particular attention to the sentence structures.

It is Halloween. I am a princess and my son Danny is a ghost. I carry his orange pumpkin bucket around and wear a tiara on my head. Danny isn't saying anything but that's because ghosts don't talk. I collect pink Kit Kats from Mrs Levinger and lollipops from Mr Cruz. I ask Danny if he wants anything but he's too good at being a ghost. When Mrs Rachel, Danny's violin teacher, sees me at the door, she takes me in an embrace. She doesn't see him in his costume. She only sees the headlines – missing boy – on the news.

Erinn Pascal

1.6

Check for understanding

1 Circle which of the following sentence structures are used in the story.

sentence fragments simple sentences **complex sentences**

varied sentence lengths repetition

2 What important information is added between the dashes in the final sentence of the story?

____

3 What is the effect of using dashes to separate the information in this sentence?

____

____

4 How does the final sentence contribute to the meaning and tone of the story?

____

____

____

complex sentence A sentence with one or more subordinate clauses. In the following example, the subordinate clause is shown in brackets: I took my umbrella [because it was raining]

1.7

Check for understanding

The following piece of flash fiction was written by a Year 9 student. It is beautifully evocative and, in only a few words, reveals an important historical **context**.

> I told my daughter stories. I spoke of ice-cream we would eat, songs we would sing. I told her lies. Cramped on a train, little stars pasted on chests, we chugged towards a future that was far from golden. So I told her golden stories, built on love and lies.
>
> Freya Cox, Year 9

context An environment or situation (social, cultural or historical) in which a text is responded to or created. Or wording surrounding an unfamiliar word, which a reader or listener uses to understand its meaning

1 What evidence is there that suggests this story is about the Holocaust?

2 The last sentence extends the idea that is introduced in the first sentence. What do you think is the effect of this approach?

3 Count the words in each sentence and write a total above each. What is the effect of varying the sentence lengths in this manner?

4 What do you think the writer means by the word 'golden' in the story?

1.8 Get creative

1 Nanofiction can also be used to tell real-life stories, like memoirs. Browse the websites www.sixwordstories.net and www.smithmag.net, reading the examples of six-word flash fiction and memoirs. You can also listen to some of the stories behind the memoirs on the second website. Record your three favourite six-word pieces below.

2 Now create your own six-word memoir (you can submit it on the www.smithmag.net website, too).

Show and tell

While authors of flash fiction have to be very selective with their words, there is still room for beautiful descriptions and interesting language in this type of writing. The classic rule for writing is 'show, don't tell', which means that writers should describe characters, settings and events in ways that allow readers to draw their own conclusions, rather than being told what to feel or think. Anton Chekhov (famous writer) famously explained, 'Don't tell me the moon is shining; show me the glint of light on broken glass.'

Showing instead of telling requires writers to carefully select words with sensory effects which create vivid images. 'Showing' will make the reader feel that they can see, hear, touch, taste or smell the elements of the story. This is a very important part of engaging your readers in flash fiction. Consider the examples below.

Examples	Showing or telling?
Indigo felt scared as she began her speech.	telling
Indigo's heart raced and her hands trembled when she saw all the faces looking at her.	showing
The house looked old and abandoned.	telling
The house sagged against the overgrown weeds, its long-broken windows like empty eye sockets.	showing

The 'show, don't tell' rule, however, needs to be all about balance: it should really be 'show *and* tell'. Some degree of 'telling' is required to supply information and to condense parts of the story. Too much showing slows down the story and may overwhelm your reader with sensory detail. Too much telling means the reader is not given space to make any inferences. Important scenes and dialogue should be 'shown', while less important moments and information should be 'told' to maintain the pace of the story.

1.9 Check for understanding

Browse the flash fiction website www.100wordstory.org or search online until you find a 100-word story that you like. Analyse the story by applying the following questions to it.

1 What is the title of the story? ______________________

2 Who is the author of the story? ______________________

3 What appealed to you about the story? Explain what you liked or found interesting about it.

____

____

4 Identify how much of the story is 'telling' and how much of the story is 'showing' by highlighting the parts of the story that use these approaches using two different colours.

5 Are there parts of the story where there is too much telling and you think the writer could have allowed readers to fill in the gaps for themselves? What advice would you offer the author if you were editing their work?

____

____

____

6 Are there parts of the story where there is too much showing and you are unsure of what is happening because not enough information is provided? Rewrite the parts of the story in your English notebook where this is the case.

____

____

Editing for length

It is no easy task to tell a whole story that engages a reader in only a few hundred words. To be successful, writers often craft a slightly longer story and then **edit** it down to be much shorter and more impactful. This process can sometimes be referred to as 'murdering [or killing] your darlings', a **phrase** coined by British writer Arthur Quiller-Couch. To 'kill your darlings' means to delete words, sentences, characters or even scenes – even if you love them – to make the story more concise and effective.

edit To prepare, alter, adapt or refine with attention to grammar, spelling, punctuation and vocabulary
phrase A group of words often beginning with a preposition but without a subject and verb combination (e.g. 'on the river'; 'with brown eyes')

1.10

Check for understanding

1 Edit down the 140-word paragraph below to exactly 50 words. Aim to appeal to an **audience** of Australian teenagers who love murder mysteries.

> That summer was the most stifling and relentless summer ever. The days were languorous and soporific and dragged on into balmy, mosquito-filled nights. The river, which was normally flat and brown, dried up completely to reveal the secrets it had hidden for aeons. Our rope swing, from which we normally leaped, shrieking, into the muddy water, stayed knotted to the dusty gum – neglected and bedraggled. The black crows croaked menacingly at the screamingly noisy cicadas. The grass grew crunchy and sharp under our soft, bare feet; the bitumen was sticky-hot and created shimmering heatwaves on the road. Our faces, necks and

shoulders were constantly burned and peeling as we played under the beating sun. It was on the penultimate day of one idyllic week of joy, when the final hints of moisture dried in the riverbed, that we noticed the skull.

2 Compare your new paragraph with that of a partner. Did you edit in a similar way or did you make different creative decisions? Note your comparisons below.

3 Circle all the words below that you think best describe the **style** of flash fiction writing.

economical	succinct	condensed
concise	longwinded	brief
verbose	wordy	restrained
controlled	selective	repetitive
sparing	measured	

audience An intended or assumed group of readers, listeners or viewers that a writer, designer, filmmaker or speaker is addressing

style The distinctive language features, text structures and/or subject matter in a text which may shape meaning, be enjoyed for its aesthetic qualities or distinguish the work of an author, period etc.

Engaging with evaluation

What is the best film you've ever seen? What's the worst? What about the silliest idea you've ever heard, or a social issue you have a strong opinion on? We naturally form judgements about just about every experience or idea that we encounter. Every time we write about our experiences or opinions in ways that share these personal judgements, we are creating evaluative texts. These texts include letters to the editor, talkback radio, podcasts, social media comments and online reviews. This unit will help you to understand how language works in these written evaluative texts to communicate judgements and to influence the audience.

In this unit you will learn:

- how evaluation can be expressed directly and indirectly
- how language features are used to express a perspective
- to communicate your own evaluations.

Curriculum content

Australian Curriculum content description	Content code
Understand how evaluation can be expressed directly and indirectly using devices such as allusion, evocative vocabulary and metaphor.	AC9E9LA02
Analyse and evaluate how language features are used to represent a perspective of an issue, event, situation, individual or group.	AC9E9LY03

Evaluation: what is it?

An evaluation is a judgement of something. You might judge how well a film has been made, or how good the food at a restaurant is, or whether you agree with a decision made by your local council. Therefore, evaluative texts are those that offer an appraisal or an assessment of something's worth or merit.

purpose An intended or assumed reason for a type of text

2.1 Reflecting and discussing

Discuss the following questions in pairs, in small groups or with the whole class as directed by your teacher.

1. When was a time you made an evaluation or judgement about something?
2. What do you think the **purpose** of an evaluative text is?
3. When do we use the word 'judge' in our daily lives?
4. We are often taught *not* to 'judge a book by its cover' or pass judgement on people's appearance. Why do you think so many evaluative texts exist when the word 'judge' often has such negative meaning in our society?

Letters to the editor

A 'letter to the editor' is a letter about a topic of public interest sent to a publication, such as a newspaper or magazine, from a reader. The letters are written for the purpose of being published, so the target audience is not only the editor but also the wider readership of the publication.

A letter to the editor often express the letter writer's opinion in support of or in opposition to an opinion previously communicated in the publication by a journalist or in an editorial. Letters to the editor often comment on current issues in the media and frequently respond to previously published letters on the same topic. Read the example of a letter to the editor of a newspaper below.

Pumped Up and Ready to Pop

We cannot expect young sports stars to behave like 'normal' people when they are treated as superheroes or valiant warriors by their leagues.

Anastasia Di Stasio ('Give the Boys a Chance', 24/6) is right to slam the antisocial shenanigans of young AFL, tennis, rugby and cricket stars, but she missed laying the blame on the real culprits. The young blokes' 'massive egos' are pumped up to bursting point by the adoration and money thrown at them by the public, the media and big business.

How can we expect a 20-year-old boy to cope with being made to feel like an invincible god? Or that their talents are much more valuable to society than anyone else's? These kids are pumped up to such an extent that we shouldn't be surprised when one of them pops.

The fans, the clubs and the media have to take their fair share of the responsibility for the muscle-bound maniacs they have created. It's never acceptable to swear at umpires and disrespect the basic rules of society. This behaviour isn't made okay just because they are good at running with a ball.

Madison Das, Gardenvale

2.2 Check for understanding

phrase A group of words often beginning with a preposition but without a subject and verb combination (e.g. 'on the river'; 'with brown eyes')

1 What was your first impression or thought when you read the headline 'Pumped Up and Ready to Pop'?

2 What social issue is the writer commenting on?

3 What evidence is there that the writer is adding to a debate that has already been written about in the newspaper?

4 Who is the writer blaming for sports stars' bad behaviour?

5 Why do you think the writer uses the description 'valiant warriors'? What ideas or feelings are normally associated with the word 'warriors'?

6 What does the **phrase** 'just because they are good at running with a ball' suggest about Das' opinion of sport?

7 Is your own judgement of sportspeople influenced by their behaviour off the field? Do you think they should be held to a higher standard of behaviour because they are in the public eye?

Evaluative text structures

There are many different ways in which writers can choose to organise their ideas when they are presenting an evaluation and trying to persuade their audience to agree with it. For instance, they might start with their strongest idea or by rebutting an opposing evaluation. In the diagram below, the key points of Das' argument from the letter have been summarised to show you the order of the ideas.

Paragraph 1
- states her contention (argument) : that young sportspeople are not entirely to blame for their poor behaviour

Paragraph 2
- refers to the article and writer she is replying to
- agrees with the main point of the other argument
- gives reasons she thinks sportspeople are not entirely to blame

Paragraph 3
- places blame on the attitudes of fans, clubs and sponsors
- belittles the importance of sport in society

2.3

Check for understanding

1 Circle the words in the list below that describe the **tone** or feeling expressed in the opening sentence. Use a dictionary if required.

forthright	hedging	determined
ambivalent	blunt	subtle
definite	unsure	

2 Provide definitions for two words in the list above that you didn't know, or add synonyms for two words and define them.

____

____

3 The language used to describe players in the first two paragraphs of the letter is less critical than the language used in the last paragraph. What do you think is the effect of sequencing the use of language in this way?

____

____

tone The mood created by the language features used by an author and the way the text makes the reader feel

Evaluative language

Evaluative language includes the positive or negative words and phrases that indicate the writer's judgement of the worth of something. It includes language that expresses feelings, **attitudes** and opinions, and language that assesses the quality of the ideas and features of texts.

We might use this type of evaluative language in a very obvious way, such as describing a novel as 'fascinating and enthralling', or we might use it more subtly, implying that a city is unattractive by describing it as 'sprawling and smog-filled'. These evaluative words make meaning through connotations; that is, they make us respond emotionally through the associated meanings they evoke.

evaluative language Positive or negative language that judges the worth of something. It includes language to express feelings and opinions; make judgements; and assess quality of objects, ideas and features of texts
attitudes Particular ways of thinking and feeling towards people or things

2.4 Check for understanding

Certain connotative words in the letter by Das are used to make readers feel sorry for sportspeople and angry with those who encourage or enable their inappropriate behaviour.

Decide whether the following words evoke positive or negative connotations – or associations – by placing them in the correct columns in the table below.

agreeable introverted bold
aggressive confident arrogant
conspire cunning clever

Positive	Negative

2.5 Check for understanding

1 Find the following words and phrases in the letter and write down their meanings.

a culprits: ______

b shenanigans: ______

c invincible: ______

2 Record the words in the letter that make us feel sorry for the sportspeople.

______

______

3 Record the words that make us feel critical of those who, according to Das, cause sportspeople to behave badly.

______

______

In addition to connotative words, allusion, similes and metaphors can also help to provide an evaluation of something and direct readers to respond in particular ways. The table below illustrates their effects using examples from the letter to the editor.

Language features	Definitions	Examples from letter	Effects on reader
allusion	an indirect reference to a person, character, event, idea or other text	'... are treated as superheroes'	Readers familiar with pop culture superheroes understand that they are admired and revered, so they recognise that sportspeople being treated like superheroes is excessive and misplaced.
simile	a figurative device that compares two things using the words 'like', 'as' or 'than'	'How can we expect a 20-year-old boy to cope with being made to feel like an invincible god?'	The simile emphasises how inexperienced and ill-equipped a young 20-year-old sports star is compared with an 'invincible god', positioning readers to recognise that this is an unfair expectation on sportspeople to be perfect.
metaphor	a figurative device that compares two things by asserting one thing is another or through implicit comparison to something with similar characteristics	'... we shouldn't be surprised when one of them pops'	The metaphorical description of pressure building in a balloon until it bursts emphasises the pressure that sportspeople are under to perform perfectly.

Creating tone

Evaluative language contributes to the tone of a text by revealing a writer's judgement or opinion on the topic. The table below contains words that might indicate that an author is adopting a positive, neutral or negative tone towards the subject of their text.

Positive	Neutral	Negative
supportive	careful	accusing
accepting	restrained	critical
understanding	measured	mocking
sympathetic	calm	outraged
admiring	balanced	contemptuous

Das' tone in the letter is mostly sympathetic towards the players and critical of the society that celebrates them. The word choices reveal her attitude in sometimes subtle ways.

2.6 Reflecting and discussing

Discuss the following questions in pairs, in small groups or with the whole class as directed by your teacher.

1 What does it mean to be accused of bringing a sport into disrepute?
2 What are some examples of a sport being brought into disrepute from the news?
3 Do you agree with the evaluation offered by Das? Give reasons for your answer.
4 How does the situation of sportspeople differ from or reflect that of other celebrities like actors, musicians or social media influencers?

Annotating language features

To analyse the **language features** in an evaluative text, it can be helpful to annotate the text so that you can clearly see how the writer is using evaluative language.

'Annotation' is the process of highlighting and writing brief notes or observations around a text, such as above certain words or in the text's margins. This process will help you to pay attention to the language used, to consider the meanings and the tone created by the language and to be aware of the sequence in which particular aspects of the language are presented.

Consider the following response to Das' letter. It has been annotated to summarise the contention, show the sequence of the main points and identify the use of evaluative language.

language features Features that support meaning e.g. clause- and word-level grammar, vocabulary, figurative language, punctuation, images. Choices vary for the purpose, subject matter, audience and mode or medium

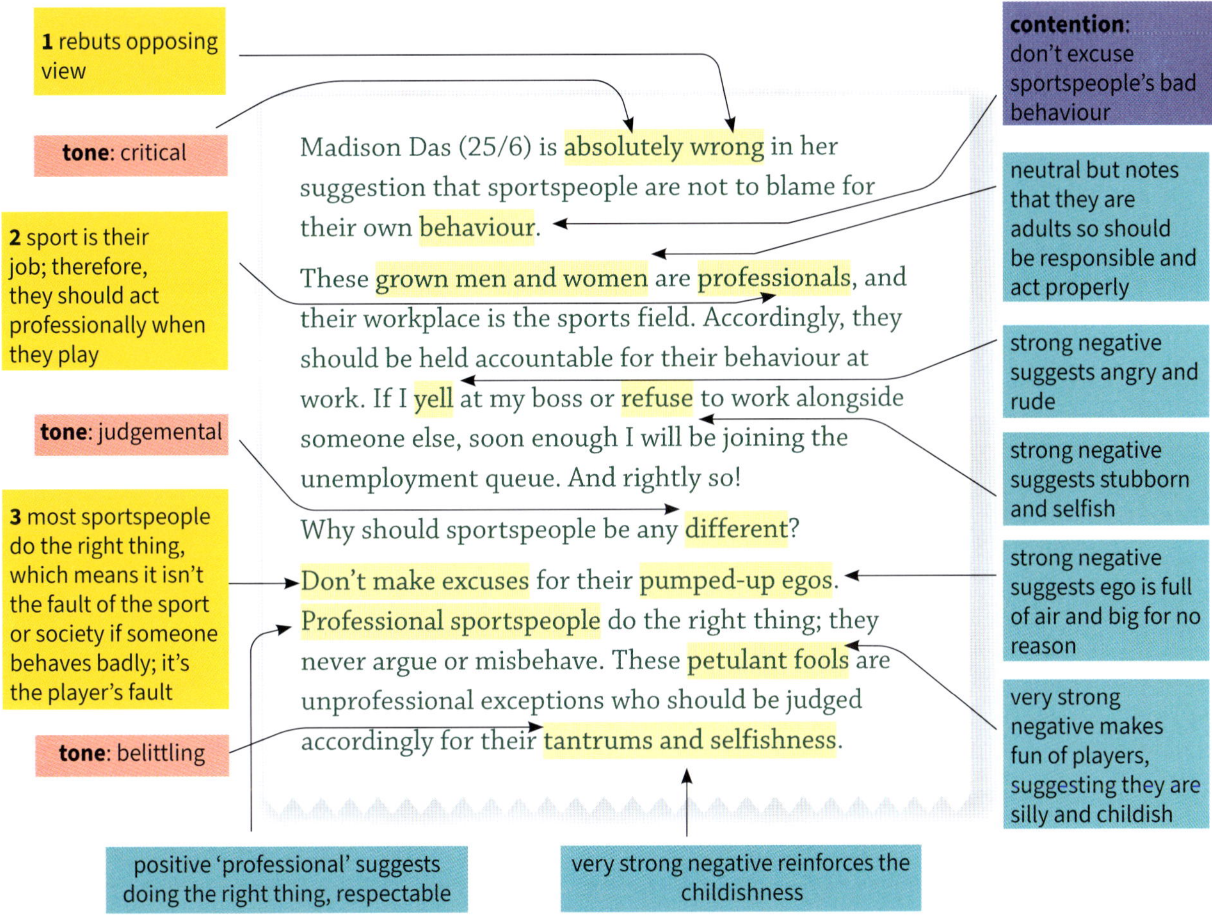
Madison Das (25/6) is absolutely wrong in her suggestion that sportspeople are not to blame for their own behaviour.

These grown men and women are professionals, and their workplace is the sports field. Accordingly, they should be held accountable for their behaviour at work. If I yell at my boss or refuse to work alongside someone else, soon enough I will be joining the unemployment queue. And rightly so!

Why should sportspeople be any different?

Don't make excuses for their pumped-up egos. Professional sportspeople do the right thing; they never argue or misbehave. These petulant fools are unprofessional exceptions who should be judged accordingly for their tantrums and selfishness.

2.7 Check for understanding

1 Annotate the following letter using the steps below.

a Highlight the contention.

b Number the key reasons or points made by the writer.

c Highlight and make notes about the evaluative language used and the tone it creates.

> Let's give these kids a break. They are normal people who work hard at their jobs and follow punishing training regimes, all for our entertainment.
>
> Every normal teenager will blow off a little steam from time to time when they get frustrated and angry. Considering the high-pressure, high-performance environment of international sport, it's surprising there isn't more dummy-spitting.
>
> The shouting behaviour-police should cut our sporting superstars some slack. Stop expecting them to be faultless angels.

2.8

Get creative

1 Write your own letter to the editor outlining your thoughts on the issue of sportspeople behaving badly or another issue that you have identified.

2 Highlight the evaluative language used within your letter.

Other evaluative texts

While this unit has concentrated mostly on letters to the editor as examples of evaluative texts, many other forms of written evaluation exist too. For instance, the comments sections in online news sources and on social media platforms also offer judgements about things in the form of reviews. They are similar to letters to the editor, but the comments are often shorter, there is more immediate interaction between commenters, and comments might not receive the same level of editing or vetting.

Read the two examples of online comments below, noting how they use evaluative language that influences an audience.

- 'Had an amazing experience at this place last night. The food was absolutely delicious and the service was top-notch. Highly recommend giving this place a try!'
- 'Unfortunately, I had a disappointing dining experience here last week. The food was mediocre at best, and the service was slow. Wouldn't recommend this place.'

2.9

Reflecting and discussing

Discuss the following questions in pairs, in small groups or with the whole class as directed by your teacher.

1 Do you ever contribute to online comments that offer a judgement about something, or do you read other people's comments?

2 What do you think are the positive and negative aspects of being able to share evaluative comments online?

3 Decide whether the following texts could be considered evaluative. If so, what is being judged and by whom?

   a an Uber driver rating

   b an advertising campaign aimed at stopping road deaths

   c an online review of a hotel

   d a promotional poster created by Tourism Australia

   e a political cartoon mocking the behaviour of a government minister

Investigating genre: Gothic literature

Do you know the story of *Frankenstein*? What about *Dracula*? Have you ever watched *The Addams Family* or its more recent spin-off, *Wednesday*? If so, you are already familiar with examples of Gothic literature and its various adaptations, transformations and influences in popular culture. Gothic literature is a genre of writing that involves elements of horror and the supernatural. This unit will help you to investigate the origins and features of Gothic literature, as well as to appreciate the aesthetic qualities of these works. You will also analyse examples of Gothic literature and multimodal adaptations of the genre.

In this unit you will learn:

- about the features of Gothic literature and its translation into film
- to analyse the effect of text structures, language features and literary devices
- to evaluate the aesthetic qualities and appeal of an author's literary style.

Curriculum content

Australian Curriculum content description	Content code
Analyse texts and evaluate the aesthetic qualities and appeal of an author's literary style.	AC9E9LE04
Analyse the effect of text structures, language features and literary devices such as extended metaphor, metonymy, allegory, symbolism and intertextual references.	AC9E9LE05

The origins and evolution of the Gothic genre

The Gothic genre became popular in the late eighteenth to early nineteenth century in England with the rise of Romanticism. Romanticism was an intellectual, literary and artistic movement or era which valued emotions over logic and reason, nature over cities and progress, and freedom and spontaneity over strict social rules. Many of the most famous Gothic writers combine these Romantic **values** with dark and unexplained mysteries. The atmosphere created in Gothic fiction is usually one of fear and a sense of foreboding.

values Ideas and beliefs specific to individuals and groups

3.1 Reflecting and discussing

Discuss the following questions in pairs, in small groups or with the whole class as directed by your teacher.

1 What does the word 'Gothic' make you think of?

2 What is your understanding of the following Gothic elements? Describe what you know about them.

a Gothic clothing

b Gothic architecture

c Gothic fiction

Gothic fiction is sometimes called 'Gothic horror'. But Gothic literature is not just about frightening readers; many stories in the genre also express an underlying moral or message about the dangers of technological progress and the consequences of trying to 'play god'.

Gothic literature has evolved and changed over the years since it first emerged. Not only have the early versions often been adapted into films or comical parodies, but the genre has been influenced by other **contexts** too. Now the genre includes variations like American Gothic, Australian Gothic, Aboriginal Gothic and suburban Gothic.

context An environment or situation (social, cultural or historical) in which a text is responded to or created. Or wording surrounding an unfamiliar word, which a reader or listener uses to understand its meaning

Features of the Gothic genre

Novels, short stories, poems and films that belong to this genre have several features in common. These include:

The following extract comes from Elizabeth Gaskell's Gothic short story 'The Old Nurse's Story', which was published in 1852.

> As winter drew on, and the days grew shorter, I was sometimes almost certain that I heard a noise as if someone was playing on the great organ in the hall. I did not hear it every evening; but, certainly, I did very often, usually when I was sitting with Miss Rosamond, after I had put her to bed, and keeping quite still and silent in the bedroom. Then I used to hear it booming and swelling away in the distance. The first night, when I went down to my supper, I asked Dorothy who had been playing music, and James said very shortly that I was a gowk to take the wind soughing among the trees for music; but I saw Dorothy look at him very fearfully, and Bessy, the kitchen maid, said something beneath her breath, and went quite white.

3.2 Check for understanding

1 Find definitions for the following words.

a gowk: ______

b soughing: ______

2 How many of the Gothic genre features in the previous diagram can you identify in the extract from Gaskell's story? List them here.

______

______

______

3 Circle the words below that describe the kind of atmosphere or mood that is created in the extract. Use a dictionary to help if necessary.

lighthearted carefree ominous foreboding

tense peaceful buoyant

4 Explain the effect of the following elements in creating this atmosphere.

a the first-person narration

______

______

b long, descriptive sentences

______

______

c other characters' reactions to the narrator's question

______

______

The vocabulary of the Gothic

The mood and atmosphere of any **narrative** is influenced by the specific words used to describe the setting and develop the plot. In Gothic literature, establishing a mysterious, unsettling mood is essential to the success of the story.

narrative The selection and sequencing of events or experiences, real or imagined, to tell a story to entertain, engage, inform and extend imagination, typically using an orientation, complication and resolution

The words listed in the following table were all taken from *The Castle of Otranto* by Horace Walpole, published in 1764. It is considered to be the first Gothic novel. The words are categorised according to the mood or atmosphere they create in the novel.

mystery	diabolic, enchantment, ghost, haunted, infernal, magician, miracle, necromancer, omens, ominous, portent, preternatural, prodigy, prophecy, secret, sorcerer, spectre, spirits, strangeness, talisman, vision
fear, terror or sorrow	afflict, agony, anguish, apprehensive, commiseration, despair, dismal, dismay, dread, fearing, fright, grief, hopeless, horrid, horror, lamentable, melancholy, miserable, mournfully, panic, sadly, scared, shrieks, sorrow, sympathy, tears, terrible, terror, unhappy, wretched
urgency	anxious, breathless, flight, frantic, haste, impatient, impetuosity, precipitately, running, sudden

3.3

Check for understanding

1 Highlight any words in the table above that are unfamiliar to you.

2 Select five or more of your highlighted words. Look up their meanings and use them in a long, descriptive sentence that creates a mysterious, unsettling mood.

a words: ____________________

b sentence: ____________________

____

____

Text structures and literary devices

Gothic literature often makes use of text structures and literary devices such as extended **metaphor**, **metonymy**, allegory, symbolism and **intertextual references**. The effects of these devices are wide and varied. They can include creating an atmosphere, representing an idea, fulfilling a symbolic function or evoking a particular emotional response from a reader or viewer. Read the following definitions in the table and their accompanying Gothic literature examples.

metaphor A type of figurative language used to describe a person or object through an implicit comparison to something with similar characteristics
metonymy A use of the name of one thing or attribute of something to represent something larger or related (e.g. using the word 'Crown' to represent a monarch of a country)
intertextual references Associations or connections between one text and other texts that may be overt or less explicit. They can take the form of direct quotation, parody, allusion or structural borrowing

Literary devices	Definitions	Gothic examples
extended metaphor	a structural approach in which a metaphor stretches over many lines or paragraphs or through a whole text	The ruined, crumbling mansion in 'The Fall of the House of Usher' by Edgar Allan Poe works as an extended metaphor that represents the destruction of the Usher family.
metonymy	the use of something, or an attribute of something, to represent something larger or related	The monster created by Mary Shelley's character Victor Frankenstein can be interpreted as a metonym for the dangers of scientific and technological progress.
allegory	a story that conveys a parallel meaning or moral teaching	*Frankenstein* works as an allegory of the story of Prometheus from Greek mythology, who unwisely tried to 'play god'.
symbolism	the use of one object, person or situation to signify or represent another, by giving it meaning different from its literal meaning	The landmark rock in *Picnic at Hanging Rock* by Joan Lindsay symbolises the mystical power of nature and the Australian landscape.
intertextual references	associations or connections between one text and other texts that can be obvious or subtle; can include quotations, parodies and allusions	*Northanger Abbey* by Jane Austen is a satirical Gothic novel that pokes fun at and exaggerates the elements of other Gothic novels.

You may notice that literary devices such as these often work on the basis of symbolic meanings and associations. Their effect is frequently to remind us of something else, or to make us feel a certain way due to their associations.

3.4 Check for understanding

1 How is the house – usually a place of domesticity and safety – made to look monstrous in this image?

____

____

____

____

____

____

2 How does the image make connections to other texts? What other texts or storylines does it remind you of?

____

____

3 What is the symbolic meaning of the lights in the windows and doorway?

____

____

Gothic films

Gothic films contain the same **conventions**, or typical features, as written Gothic literature. In fact, Gothic films can be adaptations of novels or short stories, so they include the same mysterious settings and dark **themes** as those created in the originals. They have multiple **modes** at their disposal to create the Gothic **aesthetic**.

Gothic features can be emphasised in film using visual and auditory effects, such as dark lighting, eerie fogs and mists, and unsettling music or sound effects. Well-known Gothic films include *Frankenstein*, *Sweeney Todd* and *Sleepy Hollow*. Famous Australian Gothic films, which often characterise the landscape as a mysterious, threatening force, include *Picnic at Hanging Rock* and *Wake in Fright*.

convention An accepted practice that has developed over time and is generally used and understood (e.g. use of punctuation)
theme The main idea, concept or message of a text
mode Various processes of communication – listening, speaking, reading or viewing and writing or creating
aesthetic Concerned with a sense of beauty or an appreciation of artistic expression

Case study: *Edward Scissorhands*

Edward Scissorhands is a 1990 film directed by Tim Burton. Watch the trailer for the film, which is publicly available online.

3.5 Reflecting and discussing

Discuss the following questions in pairs, in small groups or with the whole class as directed by your teacher.

1 What Gothic features can you identify in the film's trailer?

2 What elements of other genres, such as romance or comedy, can you identify in the film's trailer?

3 How is a Gothic aesthetic constructed through features such as colour, music and imagery?

Creating atmosphere and mood

Films created in the Gothic **style** rely heavily on setting the right mood to generate fear and suspense. Dim or night-time lighting can help to create a dark and foreboding atmosphere. Camera angles help to make some characters look powerful and dangerous and others vulnerable and afraid.

The **mise en scène**, a French term meaning 'putting on stage', also plays a vital role in creating the atmosphere and mood in film. Mise en scène refers to all the elements visible within the frame of a film shot. The visual **imagery** created within the mise en scène in Gothic films is often quite eerie and unsettling.

style The distinctive language features, text structures and/or subject matter in a text which may shape meaning, be enjoyed for its aesthetic qualities or distinguish the work of an author, period etc.
mise en scène In film, the composition of a shot, including elements such as lighting, costumes, props, set design and special effects
imagery Visually descriptive or figurative language to represent things including objects, actions and ideas in ways that appeal to the senses of the reader or viewer

3.6 Check for understanding

Look at the mise en scène elements in the trailer for *Edward Scissorhands* by freezing a frame in the opening 37 seconds. Discuss what you can see with a partner, then look at the image below and answer the questions that follow.

1 What are the most striking visual elements in this frame?

____

____

2 How does the mise en scène create a particular atmosphere?

____

____

____

3 Describe how the choice of music is used to enhance the atmosphere and mood created in this part of the trailer.

____

____

Aesthetic qualities

Tim Burton, the creator of *Edward Scissorhands*, is famous for his particular directorial style. In fact, his style of filmmaking is so distinctive and recognisable that the term 'Burtonesque' is sometimes used to refer to characters or scenes from other films that imitate his body of work's particular aesthetic; -that is, its artistic quality. The aesthetic qualities and appeal of Tim Burton's film style are shaped by his characteristic approaches to elements such as:

- camera angles and shot types
- types of characters, settings and plot lines
- costuming and make-up
- music and lighting
- theatrical quality
- themes and ideas.

Tim Burton's collaborators also contribute to the aesthetic style of his films. For example, numerous Burton films feature the actors Johnny Depp and Helena Bonham Carter, and costume designer Colleen Atwood has worked with Burton for over 30 years on almost all of his films.

3.7 Check for understanding

Watch the trailers for the following films, also directed by Tim Burton, available on YouTube.

Alice in Wonderland	*Corpse Bride*	*Miss Peregrine's Home for Peculiar Children*

1 Which of the following features do you notice that all the trailers have in common?

a dim lighting ☐

b Gothic settings such as ruined mansions and graveyards ☐

c characters who might be considered different or strange ☐

d characters wearing heavy eye- make-up and dark clothing ☐

e actors Johnny Depp and Helena Bonham Carter ☐

2 Conduct some research on Tim Burton's directorial style. You may even want to research the influence of German Expressionism, an early-twentieth-century artistic movement, on his aesthetic. Record an observation from this research.

____

____

____

____

____

3 Do you like the aesthetic of Tim Burton's films? Give reasons for your answer.

____

____

____

Gothic motifs

Both written and film texts use similar vocabulary and imagery to create a sense of fear and dread. One way in which this atmosphere is created is through the use of motifs.

A 'motif' is an object, person or sound that appears regularly in a text and is used symbolically to represent a particular idea or emotion. For instance, the ominous music that accompanies Darth Vader in the *Star Wars* films is a motif that represents his powerful and dangerous nature.

Sometimes, motifs are unique to a particular text or genre. At other times, filmmakers and writers use familiar motifs that **audiences** will immediately recognise as symbolic of a bigger idea, such as birds to symbolise freedom or barred windows to symbolise entrapment.

audience An intended or assumed group of readers, listeners or viewers that a writer, designer, filmmaker or speaker is addressing

3.8

Check for understanding

Suggest what each of the following motifs might represent in a Gothic film and explain why. Think about what each one does, the way it looks or how it sounds. The first has been completed for you as an example.

Motifs	Suggested meanings and explanations
strong wind	approaching danger or trouble; howling wind blows things around and creates chaos
doors creaking on rusty hinges	
ruined buildings	
thunder and lightning	
characters trapped in a room	
baying of distant dogs or wolves	
sunrise	

3.9 Get creative

Using the image below as inspiration, compose a Gothic short story in your English notebook. Before you start writing, answer the questions below the image to help plan your story.

1 Which elements of the Gothic genre will you include in the story?

____

____

____

2 What effect do you hope these elements will have on your reader?

____

____

3 What motifs will you use in your story?

____

____

4 What are you trying to warn your reader about? A dangerous landscape? A mysterious outsider? A dangerous use of science? Or something else altogether?

____

____

Return to this plan when you have completed your story to check that you have included everything you intended to.

Assessing literary value

When we watch films and television shows or read books, we form opinions and make judgements about which ones we prefer and the reasons why. These judgements are usually subjective, meaning personal or biased. That's because they are based on our individual preferences and dislikes.

However, there are also more objective or unbiased ways of judging texts, based on the idea of literary value. In determining whether a text has literary value, ask yourself the following questions.

- » Is the text written or created in an interesting and imaginative way?
- » Does the text explore thought-provoking or important issues about human society or human nature?
- » Does the text challenge the audience to think about the world in different ways?
- » Is the text's appeal likely to stand the test of time?

Interestingly, Gothic writing in its early days was considered by many to have no literary value! The genre was considered cheap and trashy by the literary establishment, but it was still very popular with readers.

3.10 Reflecting and discussing

Discuss the following questions in pairs, in small groups or with the whole class, as directed by your teacher.

1. Why do you think famous Gothic works of literature, such as *Frankenstein*, are now widely considered to have literary value?
2. Do you think a film like *Edward Scissorhands* could be considered to have literary value? Provide reasons for your answer.
3. Who decides what has literary merit and value in our society?
4. Do you think that a person from a different time, culture or place would agree that the texts we celebrate today have literary value?
5. What is your opinion about what makes a text have value? You could survey your class and collate the results, or even ask some adults their opinions to see whether their ways of valuing texts are different from yours.

It is not always easy to decide which texts have literary value. We often rely on others, such as experts, for guidance about which texts are valuable. However, we should always be aiming to develop our own informed responses to texts.

In the twentieth century, some film critics began to argue that not only novels and written texts but certain television shows and cartoons had literary value, too, rather than merely popular appeal.

3.11

Get creative

1 What would you include in a list of qualities that a text needs in order to have literary value?

2 Create a poster listing these qualities, with examples of how they are shown in texts you have read or viewed, and display it in the classroom. Plan your poster in the space below.

Documentary film

Have you ever watched a nature documentary narrated by David Attenborough? Have you heard of the famous director Michael Moore, who makes documentaries about social issues? A documentary film aims to inform its audience about a particular topic. Unlike fictional films, which are scripted and acted, documentaries are about real-life events, people or issues. They can cover a wide range of topics, including social issues, historical events, scientific discoveries, cultural practices and biographical profiles.

In this unit you will learn:

- about the features and conventions of documentary films
- how documentary filmmakers use a combination of multimodal elements
- how documentaries offer representations and perspectives.

Curriculum content

Australian Curriculum content description	Content code
Examine how authors adapt and subvert text structures and language features by experimenting with spoken, written, visual and multimodal elements, and their combination.	AC9E9LA03
Analyse the representations of people and places in literary texts, drawn from historical, social and cultural contexts, by First Nations Australian, and wide-ranging Australian and world authors.	AC9E9LE01
Listen to spoken texts that have different purposes and audiences, analysing how language features position listeners to respond in particular ways, and use interacting skills to present and discuss opinions regarding these texts.	AC9E9LY02
Analyse and evaluate how language features are used to represent a perspective of an issue, event, situation, individual or group.	AC9E9LY03

The documentary form

Documentary films are usually created with the intention of presenting factual information in an engaging and informative way. The filmmakers use a variety of techniques to capture footage and tell their stories, including interviews with experts or people involved in the topic, archival footage, re-enactments and on-site filming. Often, they also use voice-over narration to provide contextual information and guide the **audience** through the information presented.

audience An intended or assumed group of readers, listeners or viewers that a writer, designer, filmmaker or speaker is addressing

4.1 Reflecting and discussing

Discuss the following questions in pairs, in small groups or with the whole class, as directed by your teacher.

1 What documentary films have you watched?

2 What do you think are the main differences between documentary films and fictional films?

3 Do you prefer to watch fictional films or documentary films? Give reasons for your answer.

Documentary vocabulary

The language we use to discuss documentaries is often the same language we use to describe and analyse any other film. We might comment, for example, on camera angles, shot types and auditory elements such as background music.

However, there are also a number of terms that are quite specific to the documentary film genre, including archival footage, voice-over and re-enactments. These features can also be experimented with in fictional films, but they are much more common in documentaries.

4.2 Check for understanding

Complete the following table by writing definitions for the documentary film terms. If researching definitions online, make sure you add 'documentary film' to your search terms.

Documentary vocabulary	Definitions
voice-over	
archival footage	
re-enactment	
dramatisation	
talking heads	
actuality footage	
witness testimony	
interviews	
facts and statistics	
focaliser	
cinéma-vérité	
graphics	

Examples of documentaries

There are many well-known documentary films and documentarians who make them. Read the list of examples below, then complete the activity that follows

- *Super Size Me* (2004) directed by Morgan Spurlock ________________
- *Planet Earth* (2006) narrated by David Attenborough ________________
- *Gurrumul* (2018) directed by Paul Damien Williams ________________
- *An Inconvenient Truth* (2006) directed by Davis Guggenheim ________________
- *March of the Penguins* (2005) directed by Luc Jacquet ________________
- *He Named Me Malala* (2015) directed by Davis Guggenheim ________________
- *That Sugar Film* (2014) directed by Damon Gameau ________________
- *2040* (2019) directed by Damon Gameau ________________
- *Blue* (2017) directed by Karina Holden ________________
- *I Am Eleven* (2011) directed by Genevieve Bailey ________________
- *Ladies First* (2017) directed by Uraaz Bahl ________________

4.3 Check for understanding

1 Which of the documentaries listed have you seen? If you have not seen any in this list, what other documentaries have you watched?

______

______

2 Why do you think David Attenborough is named as the narrator of *Planet Earth* when all the other examples on the list include the director's name?

______

______

3 Based on your prior knowledge of the films listed, or using clues from their titles, predict which of the following topics you think they explore. Write your predictions in the spaces provided next to the listed film titles above.

a environmental issues

b animal welfare and rights

c health and food production

d social justice

e biographical profile

4 What topics would you be interested in watching a documentary about? List them here and explain why these documentaries would be interesting to you.

______

______

______

Documentary audiences and viewing contexts

Documentary films are shown in many places, such as:

- movie cinemas
- free to air and public broadcasting television (e.g. ABC, SBS)
- cable and satellite television (e.g. Discovery Channel, History Channel)
- streaming platforms (e.g. Stan, Netflix, Amazon Prime)
- online via various internet websites (e.g. YouTube, DocPlay, Kanopy)
- educational settings (e.g. school classrooms)
- film festivals (e.g. Sundance, Melbourne International Film Festival)

This diversity in the ways in which documentaries can be viewed means that their audiences can also be widely varied, spanning a range of social groups and ages who access them in different ways.

4.4 Reflecting and discussing

Discuss the following questions in pairs, in small groups or with the whole class as directed by your teacher.

1 Where have you watched documentaries before?

2 What factors would you need to consider if you were trying to identify the target audience of a documentary (e.g. age, gender)?

What is the purpose of documentaries?

Documentaries are an important form of media because they can inform and educate viewers about topics, events, people and issues, sparking discussions and raising awareness about subjects that might not otherwise receive widespread attention.

A main **purpose** of a documentary is to represent one or more perspectives on an issue, event, situation, individual or group. Documentaries also aim to engage the audience by presenting their representations and perspectives in interesting ways through a range of communication modes.

purpose An intended or assumed reason for a type of text

4.5 Check for understanding

Select any three documentary titles from the previously listed well-known films. Watch the trailer for each title. For each film, record your impression of who its target audience might be and what its purpose is likely to be.

1 Documentary 1 title: ______________________

Audience: ______________________

Purpose: ______________________

2 Documentary 2 title: ______________________

Audience: ______________________

Purpose: ______________________

3 Documentary 3 title: ______________________

Audience: ______________________

Purpose: ______________________

Types of documentaries

Documentaries can be grouped into types based on common topics or approaches to their subject matter. There are many different types of documentaries. Some of them are listed in the table below with their definitions.

4.6 Check for understanding

Look up and add the missing definitions to the table below, then research additional types of documentaries and add them to the table together with their definitions.

Documentary types	Definitions
historical	Explores a historical event; the film may include archival footage, personal accounts and interviews with experts.
observational	Observes and documents real events and situations as they unfold; no filmmaker interference is evident.
investigative	Reveals research and investigates its topic thoroughly; the film may feature interviews and new facts aiming to uncover hidden truths or encourage action on an issue.
participatory	
biographical	

Multimodal elements

Documentary films combine different language **modes** of communication, including visual, auditory and written modes, to convey their ideas and explore their topics. For instance, a documentary might include an interview with an expert (which we listen to), a close-up camera angle on the expert (which we can see) and a written caption (which we read to discover the name and professional role of the expert).

The documentary film poster below includes two modes of communication through its **language features**: written and visual.

Tagline uses an ocean-inspired pun and creates a sense of urgency.

Centred written film title connects to the blue colour scheme and evokes association with the expression 'the deep, blue ocean'.

Several different shot types and angles combine to create the vision of a beautiful, mysterious underwater world, full of natural ocean life, and of humans interacting with it.

mode Various processes of communication – listening, speaking, reading or viewing and writing or creating
language features Features that support meaning e.g. clause- and word-level grammar, vocabulary, figurative language, punctuation, images. Choices vary for the purpose, subject matter, audience and mode or medium

4.7 Check for understanding

1 What topic is explored in the documentary that the poster above promotes?

____

2 In the following table, decide which modes the examples use by placing ticks in the relevant columns. If they use more than one mode of communication they can be considered **multimodal**, so place a tick in the final column, too.

multimodal A combination of 2 or more communication modes (e.g. print, image and spoken text, as in film or computer presentations)

Examples	Auditory (do we listen to this feature?)	Visual (do we see this feature?)	Written (do we read this feature?)	Multimodal
a caption detailing the date and location of a certain scene				
an interview with an expert				
a voice-over explanation				
a re-enactment of a past event				
background music				

4.8 Get creative

Design a multimodal documentary film poster (using visual and written elements) for one of the following hypothetical titles and descriptions of documentaries. You can plan your poster in the space provided, but you might opt to create it digitally.

1 *Invisible Chains* –: a documentary examining modern-day slavery

2 *Beyond Borders* –: a documentary exploring the experiences of refugees and asylum seekers

3 *Generation Divide* –: a documentary exploring the growing generational gap and its impact on society

Case study: *In My Blood It Runs*

In My Blood It Runs is a 2019 observational documentary directed by Maya Newell and filmed in the Northern Territory, mostly in Mparntwe (Alice Springs), Sandy Bore Homeland and the Borroloola community.

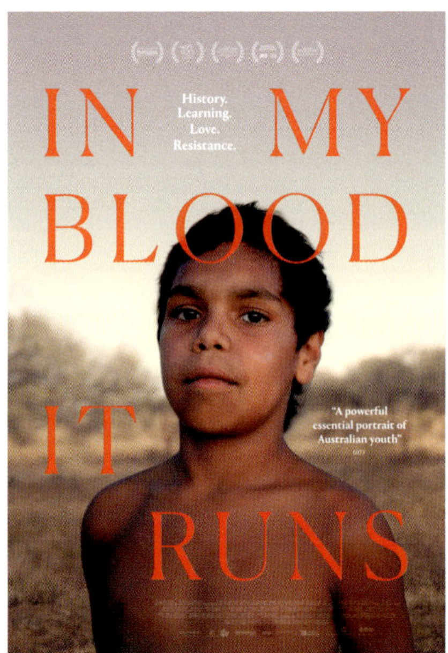

The documentary follows the life of ten-year-old Arrernte/Garrwa boy Dujuan and his family. Dujuan experiences many challenges at school as a result of prejudice against First Nations Australians and misunderstandings of First Nations cultural practices. The film reveals the importance of history, language and cultural practices to First Nations Australians.

At only 12 years old, Dujuan became the youngest person ever to address world leaders at the United Nations Human Rights Council.

Scan the QR code and watch the trailer for the film on the official website.

Note for teachers: The website for the film includes information about the making of the film, a range of educational resources including study guides, and professional learning opportunities for teachers. It is highly recommended that educators access the professional development opportunities, such as the free accredited online learning course, prior to engaging students in the viewing and study of *In My Blood It Runs*. The website provides various options for viewing the full film.

Scan the QR code to visit the official website for the film and spend some time reading through the information it provides.

4.9 Check for understanding

1 Circle which of the following documentary features are evident in the film's trailer.

archival footage   interviews   voice-over

re-enactments   cinéma-vérité

2 Why do you think the film is classified as an observational documentary?

____

____

3 Re-watch the trailer and record some of the review comments that appear as written features in the space below.

4 Based on the trailer, what **themes** do you think will be explored in the documentary?

5 How does the music in the trailer enhance its representation of the film's themes?

theme The main idea, concept or message of a text

4.10 Check for understanding

Have a close look at the official website for *In My Blood It Runs*: https://inmyblooditruns.com/

1 Record the titles of the seven tabs included on the website.

2 What social media websites does this website connect with?

3 The website explains that *In My Blood It Runs* is not just a film; it is also a campaign. What three main goals does the campaign aim to focus on?

4 Find definitions for the following words, which are all relevant to the film.

a marginalisation: ______________________________

b self-determination: ______________________________

c disempowerment: ______________________________

d ancestral: ______________________________

e Arrernte: ______________________________

5 The film highlights the way in which language connects to cultural identity. Dujuan's intellect and abilities are often overlooked or minimised by the education system. What abilities does Dujuan possess that are not valued or measured by his school?

____

____

____

Representations of people and places

Documentaries often represent people and places in a certain light in order to position audiences to respond in particular ways. While it is easy to simply argue that *In My Blood It Runs* represents Dujuan 'positively' so that audiences are positioned to like him and the school system 'negatively' so that audiences oppose it, there are much more precise and accurate ways of discussing the representations created.

4.11

Check for understanding

1 Circle the appropriate **adjectives** below to describe the way Dujuan is represented in the film. Use a dictionary to help you if necessary.

resilient   intuitive   ignorant   playful   innocent

impressionable   inspiring   intelligent   disillusioned

2 Circle the audience responses below that might be created by these representations of Dujuan. Use a dictionary to help you if necessary.

respect   defiance   admiration   empathy

anger   sympathy   understanding   compassion

3 Brainstorm some adjectives that you could use to describe the ways in which the following places are represented in the film.

a Dujuan's schools: ________________________________

b Sandy Bore, NT: ________________________________

c Hidden Valley, Mparntwe: __________________________

adjective A word class that describes, identifies or quantifies a noun or a pronoun, e.g. two (number or quantity), my (possessive), ancient (descriptive), shorter (comparative), wooden (classifying)

Representation of values

Values – what people believe are important principles or ideals – are also represented in documentaries. Dujuan's personal and cultural values of history and connection to Country are evident in the film. In fact, the film's title comes from a statement that Dujuan makes about history, which he believes is in his genetic and spiritual makeup. He says of history, 'In my blood it runs', suggesting the value and importance he places on memories and cultural heritage. These values are communicated through his keen interest in the storytelling of the elders and the Dreaming stories, and his learning of the Arrernte language.

4.12 Reflecting and discussing

Discuss the following questions in pairs, in small groups or with the whole class as directed by your teacher.

1 Why do you think history is so important to Dujuan?

2 What version of history is Dujuan taught about at school?

3 Dujuan is multilingual, meaning he knows how to speak and understand multiple languages. In the documentary, he mostly speaks Aboriginal English, but he also knows English, Garrwa and Arrernte. How many languages can you speak?

4 What does Dujuan's multilingual experience tell us about him?

5 What is the difference between Aboriginal English and the English taught at Dujuan's school?

6 What is your opinion of the film and its representations? Give reasons for why you have formed this opinion.

Representation of perspectives

A **perspective** is a lens through which the creator of a text sees the world, as well as the lens through which the audience sees the world or understands a text. For instance, perspectives include:

- a First Nations Australian perspective
- a youth perspective
- a parent's perspective
- a marginalised perspective
- an educated perspective.

perspective A lens through which the author perceives the world and creates a text, or the lens through which the reader or viewer perceives the world and understands a text

Perspectives can also include the viewpoints formed when the lens is applied. For instance, one parent's perspective on the world might lead to the viewpoint that they need to protect their child from any bad influences at all costs. Perspectives can be very individual, though. Another parent's perspective might lead to the viewpoint that some exposure to bad influences will build resilience and independence in their child.

The language features of documentaries work to represent a perspective on an issue, event, situation, individual or group. These language features can include written, visual, auditory and spoken language, as well as film language generally, like camera shots and angles. *In My Blood It Runs* represents perspectives on current issues, such as the Australian education system, juvenile detention and institutional racism. The perspectives are represented through Dujuan himself, his family and the filmmakers.

4.13 Check for understanding

1 What is Dujuan's perspective on the importance of Country and reconnecting to the 'bush'?

____

____

2 What is the filmmakers' perspective on the education of First Nations Australian students?

____

____

3 What is the perspective of Carol (Dujuan's grandmother) on learning Arrernte?

____

____

Dujuan delivered a speech to the United Nations (UN) in 2019, when he was just 12 years old. This spoken text has a different audience and purpose from those of *In My Blood It Runs*. Find a recording of Dujuan's UN address on YouTube and listen to it.

4.14 Check for understanding

1 What audience do you think *In My Blood It Runs* is made for? Consider age, nationality, gender, interests, values and **attitudes**.

____

____

2 How is the audience at Dujuan's UN address different from the audience of the film? Consider age, nationality, gender, interests, values and attitudes.

____

____

3 Dujuan can only rely on spoken language in his UN address, but a written transcript of what he said is also available. Circle the language features below that are present in his speech to the UN.

personal pronouns   repetition   rhetorical questions

anecdotes   short sentences

4 What perspectives does Dujuan offer in his UN address? Try to describe the lens through which he sees the world, as well as his viewpoints.

____

____

____

5 How might the listeners have responded to Dujuan's speech?

____

____

attitudes Particular ways of thinking and feeling towards people or things

Persuading an audience

Have you ever tried to persuade a parent or guardian to buy you something, or to let you go to a party or a concert? Have you tried to convince your friends to agree with your opinion on a topic? Chances are that you used a range of rhetorical devices and features of your voice to deliver a persuasive spoken argument in these instances. This unit will help you to communicate your opinions in the form of convincing, persuasive spoken or multimodal presentations.

In this unit you will learn:

- about rhetorical devices
- how to sequence and develop a persuasive argument using cohesive devices
- how to plan, create, rehearse and deliver spoken and multimodal presentations.

Curriculum content

Australian Curriculum content description	Content code
Investigate a range of cohesive devices that condense information in texts, including nominalisation, and devices that link, expand and develop ideas, including text connectives.	AC9E9LA04
Understand how abstract nouns and nominalisation can be used to summarise ideas in text.	AC9E9LA06
Listen to spoken texts that have different purposes and audiences, analysing how language features position listeners to respond in particular ways, and use interacting skills to present and discuss opinions regarding these texts.	AC9E9LY02
Plan, create, rehearse and deliver spoken and multimodal presentations for purpose and audience, using language features, literary devices and features of voice such as volume, tone, pitch and pace, and organising, expanding and developing ideas in ways that may be imaginative, reflective, informative, persuasive, analytical and/or critical.	AC9E9LY07

Issues and opinions

The world is full of persuasive texts in which people present their opinions on topics in the form of arguments. Persuasive speeches are a common method for delivering an argument. They can be in a number of specific forms, such as a debate, an address at a protest rally, or even a sales pitch. Persuasive speeches often respond to current issues in society. Issues, by their very nature, provoke a range of differing **perspectives**, opinions and arguments.

perspective A lens through which the author perceives the world and creates a text, or the lens through which the reader or viewer perceives the world and understands a text

5.1 Reflecting and discussing

Discuss the following questions in pairs, in small groups or with the whole class, as directed by your teacher.

1. Can you think of any famous persuasive speeches that have had a powerful effect on society?
2. What are some examples of real-life situations in which persuasive speeches are used?
3. What issues are currently being debated in society that might make good topics for persuasive speeches?
4. What are your opinions on these issues?
5. What do you think is the difference between an opinion and a fact?

What is rhetoric?

'Rhetoric' is a type of language used to persuade or influence people. The formal study of rhetoric began in Ancient Greece during the fifth century BCE, when the effective use of persuasive speech could help people to gain political power – a skill widely used by politicians to this day. A summary of common rhetorical devices is provided in the following table.

Rhetorical devices	Definitions
alliteration	repetition of initial consonant sounds in a series of words
anaphora	repetition of a word or phrase at the beginning of successive clauses or sentences
antithesis	contrasting or juxtaposing two opposing ideas in a parallel structure
appeal	a strategy that seeks to appeal to the values of an audience, such as an appeal to their sense of justice, need for safety or financial interests
call to action	an explicit appeal to the audience to change their attitude or behaviour or to carry out a particular action
direct address	use of pronouns such as 'you' and 'your' to directly address the audience

emotive language	language that has strong emotional impacts on the audience by appealing to their worries, hopes and personal values
hyperbole	exaggerated statements or claims not meant to be taken literally
inclusive diction	use of pronouns such as 'us' and 'we' to invite the audience to feel part of a group, e.g. a group that can be an important part of the solution to the problem at hand
metaphor	a figure of speech that makes a comparison between two unrelated things
parallelism	repetition of grammatical structures or patterns for emphasis and clarity
rhetorical question	a question posed for effect or to make a point rather than to elicit an answer

5.2 Check for understanding

1 Draw lines to match the following examples with the rhetorical devices used in them.

› We've said this a billion times already; we cannot afford to delay any more.	antithesis
› Education is the key that unlocks the door to a world of possibilities.	hyperbole
› In moments of darkness, we discover our own light.	parallelism
› We can strive for excellence, fight for justice and build a brighter future.	metaphor
› The importance of the safety of our children is paramount.	appeal

2 Highlight the examples of inclusive diction used in the examples above.

3 In the form of full sentences, provide your own examples of the following rhetorical devices or use existing examples from famous speeches. You may need to conduct some research.

a alliteration:

____

____

b anaphora:

____

____

c call to action:

____

____

d direct address:

____

____

e emotive language:

____

____

f rhetorical question:

____

____

Former Australian Prime Minister Paul Keating's 'Redfern Speech' (December 1992) is considered one of the most important speeches in recent Australian history. Keating used many examples to support his central argument and to remind his audience – the people of Australia – of the impacts of colonisation on First Nations Australians.

Read aloud the following extract from the speech opening or scan the QR code and watch it in full.

> We non-Aboriginal Australians should perhaps remind ourselves that Australia once reached out for us. Didn't Australia provide opportunity and care for the dispossessed Irish? The poor of Britain? The refugees from war and famine and persecution in the countries of Europe and Asia? Isn't it reasonable to say that if we can build a prosperous and remarkably harmonious multicultural society in Australia, surely we can find just solutions to the problems which beset the first Australians – the people to whom the most injustice has been done.
>
> And, as I say, the starting point might be to recognise that the problem starts with us non-Aboriginal Australians.
>
> It begins, I think, with the act of recognition. Recognition that it was we who did the dispossessing. We took the traditional lands and smashed the traditional way of life. We brought the disasters. The alcohol. We committed the murders. We took the children from their mothers. We practised discrimination and exclusion.
>
> It was our ignorance and our prejudice. And our failure to imagine these things being done to us. With some noble exceptions, we failed to make the most basic human response and enter into their hearts and minds. We failed to ask –, how would I feel if this were done to me?

5.3

Check for understanding

1 Highlight the examples of inclusive diction in the extract.

2 Who do you think Keating means by 'we' in the speech?

____

3 Record an example of a rhetorical question used in the speech.

____

4 Find an example of emotive language used in the speech. Record it below and explain what kind of emotional response the audience is likely to react with.

____

____

____

5 Why do you think the speech is considered to be so important?

____

____

____

Sentence fragments, nominalisation and abstract nouns

'Sentence fragments' are parts of sentences that do not contain both a subject and a **verb**, so they can sometimes be considered grammatically incorrect. However, in creative responses, including persuasive speeches, fragments can be used to create a grammatical pause, inviting us to reflect on the idea we've just read or heard before we move on to the next idea. Look closely at the following examples of sentence fragments from Paul Keating's speech.

- 'The poor of Britain? The refugees from war and famine and persecution in the countries of Europe and Asia?'
- 'Recognition that it was we who did the dispossessing.'

Sometimes, speech writers also convey their ideas using nominalisation or abstract nouns –; that is, they turn a verb or **adjective** into a **noun**. For instance, Paul Keating nominalises the verbs 'to discriminate' and 'to exclude' to 'discrimination' and 'exclusion'. Nominalisation has the effect of making writing and speaking more concise by reducing the number of **clauses** needed.

noun A word class that includes all words denoting person, place, object or thing, idea or emotion. Nouns may be common, proper, collective, abstract and compound
verb A word class that expresses processes that include doing, feeling, thinking, saying and relating
adjective A word class that describes, identifies or quantifies a noun or a pronoun, e.g. two (number or quantity), my (possessive), ancient (descriptive), shorter (comparative), wooden (classifying)
clause A grammatical unit referring to a happening or state — e.g. 'the team won' (happening), 'the dog is red' (state), usually containing a subject and a verb group/phrase

5.4

Check for understanding

1 Find and record another example of a sentence fragment from the extract.

____

2 What word is nominalised in the following line: 'It begins, I think, with the act of recognition.'

____

3 The speech includes lots of abstract nouns which work to summarise complex ideas that are intangible. Abstract nouns are different from common nouns because they represent things that cannot be seen, smelled, heard or touched as concrete objects. Record a list of abstract nouns used in the speech extract.

____

____

Purpose and audience

The **audiences** of persuasive speeches are never just 'everyone'. While speeches might be listened to by people who are not the intended audience, they are generally delivered within a particular **context** to a specific audience who share the same characteristics as each other, such as age, interests, **values** or backgrounds. Effective speeches target their audience through the use of carefully chosen language, rhetorical devices and examples appropriate to them. Examples of intended audiences are:

» students at a high school
» attendees at a political or protest rally
» residents of a city.

audience An intended or assumed group of readers, listeners or viewers that a writer, designer, filmmaker or speaker is addressing
context An environment or situation (social, cultural or historical) in which a text is responded to or created. Or wording surrounding an unfamiliar word, which a reader or listener uses to understand its meaning
values Ideas and beliefs specific to individuals and groups

Likewise, the **purpose** of a persuasive speech is more specific than just wanting to persuade an audience in a general sense. It may be to persuade them to take action on an issue, to change their behaviour or to alter their attitude towards something. Examples of intended purposes are:

» to encourage people to write to their local member of parliament about an issue
» to challenge people to rethink their attitude towards the elderly population
» to prompt people to call out cyberbullying by reporting it to authorities.

purpose An intended or assumed reason for a type of text

5.5 Reflecting and discussing

Discuss the following questions in pairs, in small groups or with the whole class, as directed by your teacher.

1 Who do you think is the specific target audience of Paul Keating's 'Redfern Speech'? What shared age groups, backgrounds, interests and values might they have? You may need to conduct some research about the context in which the speech was delivered.

2 What do you think is the specific purpose of the speech?

Sequencing and developing an argument

Many persuasive speeches present a range of points to support their argument. The order in which these points are sequenced can vary quite a lot. A popular approach is to start with an opening hook to engage the audience, to include examples and supporting evidence to back up various points in the body of the argument, and then to conclude with a call to action. Some possible ways to structure the body of a speech are:

» comparison/contrast: outline the topic, examine alternatives including their similarities and differences, then advise which choice is preferable

» three-point structure: outline the argument and provide three main points that support it, then give a conclusion that reiterates the main argument

» problem–solution: outline a problem and propose a solution that deals with it

» cause and effect: establish the connection between a specific event or situation and the effects or consequences that it leads to.

Connectives

Writers of convincing persuasive texts like speeches structure their arguments using strong connectives. **Connectives** are words and **phrases** used to introduce new ideas, link ideas together, or show similarity or difference between ideas. They are an important part of presenting an opinion because they help create **cohesion** within a text and allow the audience to follow an argument from one point to the next. The following tables include some examples of connectives and the purposes they fulfil in a paragraph.

connective Words linking, and logically relating ideas to one another, in paragraphs and sentences indicating relationships of time, cause and effect, comparison, addition, condition and concession or clarification
phrase A group of words often beginning with a preposition but without a subject and verb combination (e.g. 'on the river'; 'with brown eyes')
cohesion Grammatical or lexical relationships that bind different parts of a text together and give it unity. It is achieved through devices such as reference, substitution, repetition and text connectives

Purpose: to add a new point or expand on an existing point		
In addition, ...	As well as ...	Equally, ...
Furthermore, ...	Moreover, ...	In the same way, ...

Purpose: to introduce another side of the argument		
Some people believe ...	Despite the facts ...	Another opinion is ...
There are those who argue that ...	In contrast, ...	Contrary to this view is ...

Purpose: to refute (challenge) opposing opinions and arguments		
Despite opinions that ...	Regardless of other views, the reality is that ...	Even so, ...
Nevertheless, it is clear ...	However, on close examination ...	In any case, the fact is ...

The conclusion of a speech needs to reiterate the opinion offered and outline exactly what response is being sought from the audience. It may present a call to action. It should make clear what the audience should now think, feel or do.

Purpose: to suggest a conclusion has been reached and presented		
It must, therefore, be clear ...	No sensible person could disagree ...	In summary, ...
There can surely be no doubt that ...	It is ultimately clear that ...	Finally, ...

5.6

Check for understanding

Add connectives from the lists above to the examples below. The purpose of each connective is in parentheses at the end of each example.

1 ____________________ power prices are continuing to grow to meet renewable energy targets. (to add a new point or expand on an existing point)

2 I know that not all families can afford the cost of solar panels; ____________________, the bigger picture is too important for us to ignore. (to refute opposing opinions and arguments)

3 ____________________ the time to accept new energy options has arrived. (to offer a conclusion)

Features of voice

Many persuasive speeches are effective because their speakers use features of voice that have a powerful effect on audiences. Features of voice include volume, pitch, tone, pace, inflection and articulation. Control of voice in public speeches is called 'oration', and some speakers become so outstanding at the control of their voice that they build a reputation as expert orators.

5.7

Check for understanding

1 Locate definitions for the following features of voice and explain why they are important aspects of persuasive speeches.

a volume or vocal projection

Definition: ______________________________

Importance: ______________________________

____

b pitch

Definition: ______________________________

Importance: ______________________________

____

c pace

Definition: ______________________________

Importance: ______________________________

____

d pause

Definition: ______________________________

Importance: ______________________________

____

e tone

Definition: ______________________________

Importance: ______________________________

____

f inflection

Definition: ______________________________

Importance: ______________________________

____

g articulation

Definition: ______________________________

Importance: ______________________________

____

2 Choose a famous speech from the list below or look at another important speech of your choice. The speeches below and their transcripts are available to listen to and read online. Watch your chosen speech, then answer the questions below.

» Martin Luther King's 'I have a Dream' speech
» Malala Yousafzai's UN address
» Emma Watson's UN address on gender equality
» Aung San Suu Kyi's 'Freedom from Fear' speech
» Kevin Rudd's 'Sorry' speech (National Apology)
» Stan Grant's 'Racism Is Destroying the Australian Dream' debate speech

a Who is the speaker? ______________________________

b When and where was the speech delivered? ______________________________

c What is the topic of the speech? ______________________________

d Who was the audience of the speech? ______________________________

e What rhetorical devices does the speaker use?

____

____

____

f What features of voice does the speaker use well?

____

____

g Effective speakers also use body language and eye contact in their oration. How well has the speaker used these elements in your selected speech?

____

____

h Do you agree with the speaker's argument? Provide reasons for your answer.

____

____

____

Visual elements

Sometimes, spoken persuasive texts like speeches can be enhanced with the use of visual stimuli that help to support an argument. Pictures, charts, illustrations, photographs and props can have strongly persuasive effects.

For instance, if you are delivering a speech on global warming or plastic in our oceans, you might include an infographic or emotive image like the ones here that may appeal to your audience's sense of logic or to their emotions. You might even bring in a collection of discarded plastic gathered from your waterway to support your point that plastic litter is negatively affecting ocean life.

5.8 Reflecting and discussing

Discuss the following questions in pairs, in small groups or with the whole class, as directed by your teacher.

1 Why do you think the images would be a good addition to a persuasive speech?

2 What other visual or auditory elements could be added to a persuasive speech to make it multimodal?

3 What do you think is the benefit of adding **multimodal** elements to a persuasive speech?

multimodal A combination of 2 or more communication modes (e.g. print, image and spoken text, as in film or computer presentations)

5.9 Get creative

Plan, create, rehearse and deliver a spoken or multimodal presentation by following the steps below. Record responses to the questions in your English notebook where appropriate to assist with your preparation.

1 Select an issue that is important to you as the topic of your persuasive speech.

2 Research your topic carefully, taking notes about important facts, differing opinions and points that could be used to develop your argument.

3 Decide on a target audience for your speech. Consider their age, interests, backgrounds and values, as well as the context in which they might listen to the speech. These aspects can be hypothetical; you are not limited to just your peers listening to you in the classroom.

4 Consider the purpose of your presentation. What do you want your audience to actually do as a result of listening to it? How do you want them to feel or think? How do you want them to act?

5 Develop a plan for your speech. Consider one of the structural approaches discussed previously when planning.

6 Write your speech, ensuring that you use a range of rhetorical devices.

7 **Edit** your speech carefully, making sure you have considered the importance of sentence structure, nominalisation and connectives to create cohesion in your argument.

   a Do you need to add sentence fragments for emphasis and pacing?

   b Can you nominalise some of the verbs and adjectives to summarise your ideas more concisely?

   c Have you included enough connectives?

8 Consider how you might use visual stimuli, such as props or a slide show, to support your speech. Collect or prepare these if you decide to use them.

9 Rehearse your speech. Make sure you concentrate carefully on features of voice such as volume, tone, pitch and pace. It is a good idea to record a rehearsal and play it back, listening for ways to improve.

10 Develop a checklist of rhetorical devices and elements of voice that you can observe or comment on when listening to the speeches of others. You can add multimodal elements and other aspects of delivery like body language and eye contact, too.

11 Now deliver your presentation. Good luck!

edit To prepare, alter, adapt or refine with attention to grammar, spelling, punctuation and vocabulary

UNIT 6

Interpreting poetry

Poetry is an art form that uses words to paint vivid pictures, evoke emotions and convey powerful messages. Because of poetry's compact form, poets choose every word carefully to maximise its impact. Not all poetry makes use of the rhyme and regular rhythm that you might expect of traditional poetry. Instead, poets use a variety of techniques to enhance their writing. Learning to interpret these will help you to unlock the hidden meanings and beauty within poetry.

In this unit you will learn:

- about poetic devices and the effects they create
- how to analyse and interpret a poem
- what is meant by poetic style.

Curriculum content

Australian Curriculum content description	Content code
Analyse how vocabulary choices contribute to style, mood and tone.	AC9E9LA08
Analyse the representations of people and places in literary texts, drawn from historical, social and cultural contexts, by First Nations Australian, and wide-ranging Australian and world authors.	AC9E9LE01
Present a personal response to a literary text comparing initial impressions and subsequent analysis of the whole text.	AC9E9LE02
Analyse texts and evaluate the aesthetic qualities and appeal of an author's literary style.	AC9E9LE04
Analyse the effect of text structures, language features and literary devices such as extended metaphor, metonymy, allegory, symbolism and intertextual references.	AC9E9LE05

Developing an initial understanding

Judith Wright (1915–2000) was an Australian poet who wrote about many topics, ranging from the Australian landscape and animals to issues involving colonisation and gender identity. In the poem below, 'The Surfer', she captures the intimate relationship between a surfer and the sea.

When analysing a poem, it is important to identify your initial thoughts before you go on to analyse the poem thoroughly. Note the parts of Judith Wright's poem that stand out to you, as well as the ideas that come to you, as you first read it.

The Surfer
He thrust his joy against the weight of the sea;
climbed through, slid under those long banks of foam –
(hawthorn hedges in spring, thorns in the face stinging).
How his brown strength drove through the hollow and coil
of green-through weirs of water!
Muscle of arm thrust down long muscle of water;
and swimming so, went out of sight
where mortal, masterful, frail, the gulls went wheeling
in air as he in water, with delight.

Turn home, the sun goes down; swimmer, turn home.
Last leaf of gold vanishes from the sea-curve.
Take the big roller's shoulder, speed and serve;
come to the long beach home like a gull diving.

For on the sand the grey-wolf sea lies, snarling,
cold twilight wind splits the waves' hair and shows
the bones they worry in their wolf-teeth. O, wind blows
and sea crouches on sand, fawning and mouthing;
drops there and snatches again, drops and again snatches
its broken toys, its whitened pebbles and shells.

phrase A group of words often beginning with a preposition but without a subject and verb combination (e.g. 'on the river'; 'with brown eyes')

6.1

Check for understanding

1 Write down three points that capture your initial impression of the poem. You might like to consider how the surfer feels about surfing, how the sea is depicted and a striking image that caught your attention.

2 Underline some lines that stood out to you in the poem. In the margins, make brief notes about why they stood out or why you liked them.

3 What mood or feeling is created by the poem? Does it stay the same throughout the poem? Explain your response.

4 Which words and **phrases** convey the surfer's strength and skill?

5 Why do you think Judith Wright compares the surfer to the gulls 'wheeling' (swooping and circling) through the air?

6 The poem makes use of a striking image of the sea in the final stanza. What makes this image powerful? Did you find it effective? Explain your answer.

Looking at the elements of poetry

Structure

Structure incorporates several aspects of how a poem is organised. The following structural features enhance not only the development of ideas but also the reader's experience of the poem, contributing to its musicality and pace.

Structural features	Definitions
stanzas	groups of lines arranged in separate sections to focus attention on different ideas or images in each grouping
line length	the number of words or syllables in each line
enjambment	the continuation of sentences or phrases over subsequent lines of the poem
end-stopped lines	sentences or phrases that finish at the end of a line
rhyme scheme	specific patterns of rhyming words, such as ABCB (in which the second and fourth lines rhyme)
rhythm	the pace, flow or movement of a poem
metre	patterns of stressed and unstressed syllables in lines of poetry
repetition and motifs	repeated words, phrases, sounds, symbols or images throughout a poem

6.2

Check for understanding

1 'The Surfer' is divided into three stanzas, which are groups of lines (like 'verses' in a song). They function similarly to a paragraph in a prose text. Identify the focus of each stanza in the poem.

a stanza 1: ______

b stanza 2: ______

c stanza 3: ______

2 Judith Wright uses enjambment at two key points in the poem. What effects are created by her use of long, continuous lines to describe the following images?

a the surfer swimming out to sea in stanza 1

______

______

b the angry sea in stanza 3

______

______

3 Why do you think Wright repeats 'drops' and 'snatches' in the third stanza? What does this mimic?

______

______

Persona

In prose texts, like novels or short stories, we often discuss the narrator of the story, but in poetry, the speaker of a poem is referred to as the 'persona'. You should not assume that the speaker in a poem is the poet. Poets will often invent a persona who is the **voice** behind the poem. This allows poets to offer unique **perspectives** on the **subject matter** that their poems explore.

voice The distinct personality of a piece of writing; the individual writing style of the composer, created through the way they use and mix various language features (e.g. a narrative using a child's voice)
perspective A lens through which the author perceives the world and creates a text, or the lens through which the reader or viewer perceives the world and understands a text
subject matter The topic or theme under consideration

6.3 Check for understanding

1 Who do you think is the persona in the poem 'The Surfer'? Circle the correct answer below.

Judith Wright   the surfer   an unnamed observer

2 How does the persona feel about the surfer in the first stanza? How would you describe the persona's **tone**? Circle the best answer below.

scornful   bored   amused

admiring   worried   joyful

3 How does the repetition of 'turn home' in the second stanza reveal the persona's growing concern?

____

____

4 Do you think the persona is right to be concerned? What do they know that the surfer doesn't yet seem to know?

____

____

tone The mood created by the language features used by an author and the way the text makes the reader feel

Poetic devices

Poets use a range of poetic devices and techniques to create mood and convey meaning. When analysing poetry, it is important to do more than simply identify the poetic devices used by a poet. You must also consider their effect on the reader and how they help to build the meaning of the poem.

6.4

Check for understanding

1 Re-read 'The Surfer'. Find an example of each of the poetic devices defined below and explain the effect of your chosen example.

a alliteration: the repetition of initial letters, usually consonants

Example: ______________________________

Explanation: ______________________________

____

b sibilance: the repetition of the 's' sound

Example: ______________________________

Explanation: ______________________________

____

c assonance: the repetition of vowel sounds within words near each other

Example: ______________________________

Explanation: ______________________________

____

d metaphor: a figurative language device that describes one thing as though it is something else, in order to draw a comparison between the two things

Example: ______________________________

Explanation: ______________________________

____

e simile: a figurative language device in which two things are directly compared using the words 'like' or 'as'

Example: ______________________________

Explanation: ______________________________

____

f personification: a figurative language device in which a non-living or inanimate thing is given living or human qualities

Example: ______________________________

Explanation: ______________________________

____

g imagery: the use of sensory details to create an evocative picture in the reader's mind

Example: ______________________________

Explanation: ______________________________

____

2 Judith Wright develops an extended metaphor of a wolf to describe the sea in the final stanza.

a What wolf-like qualities does Wright give to the sea? ______________

b What strong **verbs** are used? ______________

c What image of the sea does this create? ______________

d How does sibilance contribute to this image? ______________

e How is this different from the depiction of the sea in the first stanza?

____

3 What comment do you think Judith Wright is making about the sea and those who surf in it? Explain your answer using evidence from the poem.

____

____

____

____

verb A word class that expresses processes that include doing, feeling, thinking, saying and relating

Developing an informed interpretation

Developing an interpretation of a poem requires multiple readings. Your initial impressions of a poem can be deepened or even challenged by your subsequent readings and analysis. As you explore the elements of a poem's construction, deeper meanings can come to light that enrich your understanding.

It is important to remember that the meanings of poems are not always obvious, and that a poem can have more than one meaning. When writing about your interpretation, it is important that you are able to support it with evidence from the text. This will make your interpretation credible (reasonable or logical).

Your first reading is about gaining an initial impression of the poem.

» What stands out to you about the poem?

» What images are created?

» What situation or experience does it seem to capture?

theme The main idea, concept or message of a text
purpose An intended or assumed reason for a type of text

Secondly, read the poem for emotion.

» What tone or atmosphere is created within the poem?

» What mood does it make you feel?

Thirdly, read the poem for meaning, brainstorming potential **themes** or messages within the poem.

» What does the poet seem to be saying about this situation or experience?

» What do you think the poet's **purpose** might be?

Next, begin your close, analytical reading, focusing on:

» structure –: Consider whether the poet uses a particular form. Examine how words are arranged into lines, and lines into stanzas.

» language –: Identify the type of language used by the poet. Consider the choice of words and the connotations, or associated meanings, they convey.

» imagery –: Note the use of sensory details to create vivid images. Consider not only visual details, but auditory (sound), olfactory (smell), tactile (touch) and even gustatory (taste) imagery.

» movement –:Identify the rhythm and pace of the poem. Reading the poem aloud can help with this.

» sounds –: Listen for the use of sound devices, such as rhyme, alliteration, assonance and onomatopoeia.

Now consider external information or prior knowledge.

» Do you know anything about the **context** of the poet or the topic of the poem?

» Can this help you interpret the poem's meaning?

Finally, re-read the poem and reflect on its effectiveness. Review your interpretation of the poem following your close analysis.

context An environment or situation (social, cultural or historical) in which a text is responded to or created. Or wording surrounding an unfamiliar word, which a reader or listener uses to understand its meaning

» Can you refine what you think its themes are?

» How do the elements of its construction contribute to the meaning?

» How effective or impactful did you find the poem?

6.5 Reflecting and discussing

Discuss the following questions in pairs, in small groups or with the whole class, as directed by your teacher.

1 Share your initial impressions of Judith Wright's poem 'The Surfer' with your group. What similarities and differences were there in people's initial thoughts on the poem?

2 Did those initial impressions change through close analysis?

3 Was the group's final understanding of the poem and its themes similar or different? Why do you think this is the case?

Rhyme and rhythm

'The Surfer' is an example of a free verse poem – a poem that does not use a regular stanza structure or rhyme scheme. Many poems, however, like 'The Road Not Taken' by Robert Frost, do make use of regular rhyme and rhythm patterns.

The Road Not Taken

Two roads diverged in a yellow wood,
And sorry I could not travel both
And be one traveler, long I stood
And looked down one as far as I could
To where it bent in the undergrowth;

Then took the other, as just as fair,
And having perhaps the better claim,
Because it was grassy and wanted wear;
Though as for that the passing there
Had worn them really about the same,

And both that morning equally lay
In leaves no step had trodden black.
Oh, I kept the first for another day!
Yet knowing how way leads on to way,
I doubted if I should ever come back.

I shall be telling this with a sigh
Somewhere ages and ages hence:
Two roads diverged in a wood, and I –
I took the one less traveled by,
And that has made all the difference.

6.6 Check for understanding

1 What do you think the forked path in the wood might symbolise?

____

2 What is significant about the fact that the persona chose the road 'less traveled by'?

____

____

3 How do you think the persona feels about their decision? What mood is captured in the poem?

____

4 How does the regularity of the rhythm and rhyme help enhance the poem's theme about the persona's journey through life?

____

____

5 This poem is written in stanzas of five lines in length, known as quintains (or sometimes quintets). Use the internet to find out the names of stanzas of different lengths and complete the following table.

Number of lines	Names of stanzas
2	
3	
4	
5	quintain or quintet
6	
7	
8	

6 Identifying the rhyme scheme in a poem requires the labelling of each line, with a different letter corresponding to each rhyme. For example, in an ABCB rhyme scheme, only the second and fourth lines rhyme. Which pattern does 'The Road Not Taken' use? Circle the correct answer.

ABBBA ABABA ABAAB ABCAB AABBA

7 The poet uses a relatively regular metre in this poem. If you read the poem aloud, emphasising where the stressed syllables fall, you should see the following pattern emerge. The '/' represents the emphasised syllables (Frost cheats slightly, as 'in a' is really two syllables).

x	/	x	/	x	/	x	/
Two	roads	di	verged	in a	yell	ow	wood

This repeated pattern of unstressed then stressed syllables is known as 'iambic' rhythm. Identify the patterns of stressed and unstressed syllables in the three other common types of rhythms below. You will need to do some research.

a trochaic: ______________________

b anapaestic: ______________________

c dactylic: ______________________

8 As the iambic pattern, or 'foot', is repeated four times in each line, this metre is called 'iambic tetrameter'. Draw lines to match the number of feet, or repetitions, in a line of poetry with the correct metre name. One has been done for you.

three feet	hexameter
four feet	trimeter
five feet	tetrameter
six feet	pentameter

Understanding poetic style

style The distinctive language features, text structures and/or subject matter in a text which may shape meaning, be enjoyed for its aesthetic qualities or distinguish the work of an author, period etc.

Literary **style** can sometimes be a difficult concept to grasp. It refers to the distinctive manner in which an author or poet uses language to convey their ideas, express their thoughts and create their literary work. You might think of it as the 'flavour' of a particular writer.

Of course, a poet's style can change over time as they mature, have new experiences or become interested in different subjects, or as particular literary trends emerge. However, by examining several works of a single writer, it is usually possible to note commonalities in the way they use language.

To identify a poet's style, you might consider the way they typically use the following elements.

A poet's style can be described in many ways. Often we characterise style in terms of its overall features, qualities, emotions or intent. When describing a poet's style, you should try to use more than one word to truly capture the 'flavour' of their poetry.

Features	Qualities	Emotions	Intentions
metaphorical	intimate	whimsical	critical
allusive	succinct	angry	satirical
narrative	vivid	melancholic	provocative
lyrical	prosaic	playful	introspective
rhythmic	evocative	romantic	elegiac

Scan the QR code for additional content relating to the style of Samuel Wagan Watson.

UNIT 7

Novel study: A Walk in the Dark

The 'coming-of-age' genre is a popular one with teenage readers. Teenagers often feel they can relate to stories of other young people exploring their identities and moving from childhood naivety to a greater understanding of the world. Jane Godwin's 2022 novel, *A Walk in the Dark*, is an example of a coming-of-age story. It features a group of five teenagers who go on an overnight trek through the Otway Ranges as part of a school expedition. They must overcome several challenges and learn a lot about each other – and themselves – along the way.

In this unit you will learn:

- about the elements that make up a narrative, such as character, setting and conflict
- how writers use language to create mood and atmosphere
- to craft a personal response to a text.

Curriculum content

Australian Curriculum content description	Content code
Analyse how vocabulary choices contribute to style, mood and tone.	AC9E9LA08
Understand punctuation conventions for referencing and citing others for formal and informal purposes.	AC9E9LA09
Present a personal response to a literary text comparing initial impressions and subsequent analysis of the whole text.	AC9E9LE02
Analyse how features of literary texts influence readers' preference for texts.	AC9E9LE03

The coming-of-age genre

The coming-of-age genre is a category of literature that explores the transition from adolescence to adulthood, capturing the challenges, self-discovery and growth experienced by young **protagonists**. This type of story is also known as a 'rite-of-passage' novel or by the German term Bildungsroman. 'Bildungsroman' means 'novel of formation', as the protagonist's identity is formed through their experiences.

Coming-of-age stories often focus on themes such as identity, independence and the search for meaning in a changing world. Through characters whom young people can relate to and familiar situations, the coming-of-age genre offers teenage readers a window into the journey of self-discovery and the complexities of navigating the transition into adulthood that they may be experiencing themselves.

protagonist The main character in a text

7.1 Reflecting and discussing

Discuss the following questions in pairs, in small groups or with the whole class, as directed by your teacher.

1 Which genre of books do you most enjoy reading? What is it about this genre that appeals to you?

2 Have you read any coming-of-age novels? Which ones? What did you think of them?

3 Why do you think readers, and teenagers especially, might appreciate reading about characters who experience challenges that they too might be experiencing?

Reading the blurb

Often, a text's appeal begins as soon as we read the blurb: the information on the back cover that gives readers an insight into what the novel is about.

A gripping and suspenseful rite-of-passage novel about five teenagers and one night that will change them all, from award-winning author Jane Godwin.

'It's just a walk in the dark. What is there to worry about?'

That's what the head teacher, Johan, says. And so the Year Nines from Otway Community School set out on an overnight hike, with no adults.

But doesn't Johan know that a storm is coming?

When five teenagers head into the forest that late afternoon, none of them is aware what the night will bring. Each will have to draw on their particular strengths to survive. Each will have to face the unknown, battling the elements, events beyond their control, and their own demons.

It's a night that will change everything.

Set in the rainforest of Victoria's Otway Ranges, *A Walk in the Dark* is about friendship, trust, identity and family, consent and boundaries, wrapped in a compulsively readable, suspense-filled adventure.

Five head into the forest, but will all five make it out?

7.2 Check for understanding

1 The blurb is designed to 'hook' potential readers. Highlight the words and **phrases** in the blurb for *A Walk in the Dark* that might encourage a reader to choose this novel.

2 '**Tone**' refers to the writer's attitude or emotion towards their subject matter. How would you describe the tone of this blurb? You can circle more than one answer.

bored	serious	excited	lighthearted
humorous	urgent	critical	enthusiastic

3 Identify three details provided in the blurb that might appeal to teenage readers in particular.

____

____

____

4 Does this blurb appeal to you personally? Give specific reasons for your answer.

____

____

____

____

phrase A group of words often beginning with a preposition but without a subject and verb combination (e.g. 'on the river'; 'with brown eyes')
tone The mood created by the language features used by an author and the way the text makes the reader feel

Characters

Characters are important elements in any story. In a coming-of-age novel, the protagonist is usually a young person who undergoes a significant transformation or transition from adolescence to adulthood. They experience a number of conflicts which, although challenging, contribute to their development and a growth in their maturity. These conflicts can be with family, friends, society or their surroundings, or they can be their own internal struggles.

It can be useful to compare characters at the end of their transformation with how they were at the beginning of the process. We can reconsider our initial impressions in light of the more informed understandings that come from gaining a deeper insight into the characters as we read the text.

In the first chapter of *A Walk in the Dark*, we learn about Chrystal, an American exchange student staying with another character, Elle. Read the following extracts, which introduce Chrystal.

Extract 1. Elle didn't suggest a shower because Chrystal never seemed to have one. Elle watched her now, sitting up in bed, twirling her hair with one hand and clutching Snoopy, the stuffed toy she was obsessed with, in the other. She hadn't brought half the clothing on the exchange packing list but she'd brought this toy. Her hair fell on her shoulders in twisted strands. It was dirty.

Extract 2. One thing that really got on Elle's nerves was that Chrystal never said please or thank you. She also never called Elle's parents by their names. And she never helped! She'd only offered one time, when she'd just got off the phone to her mum.

Extract 3.

'Would you like to borrow a watch?'

'Mmmmmm I don't wear one.'

'Do you want one for the dropping, though?'

'On account of the ticking.'

'Does the ticking bother you?'

No answer.

'This one's digital. No ticking.'

Chrystal went back to her manic texting. 'I don't wear one,' she repeated. Snoopy was wedged under her arm, her thumbs moving constantly, rapidly, across her phone. What was she doing on it all day and night? Elle wondered, and what would she do when she couldn't have it for eight hours on the hike?

Extract 4. She has such a bad diet, thought Elle, all she eats is lollies, no wonder she's so pale, and has no muscles. Elle was usually easygoing, but she was literally counting the days on her phone calendar until Chrystal would be flying back to America.

7.3 Check for understanding

Characters are developed through their description by the narrator, as well as inferences we make based on their actions, their speech and how other characters react to them.

1 Fill in the table to describe the character of Chrystal.

Physical description of Chrystal	Chrystal's actions
Chrystal's speech	Other character's reactions to Chrystal

2 Symbols can contribute to characterisation, too. Who is Snoopy? (You may need to research him on the internet.) What does Chrystal's attachment to her stuffed toy suggest about her character?

3 What are your initial impressions of Chrystal's character?

4 It is important to recognise that this representation of Chrystal is focalised, or viewed, through the character of Elle, her host student. How does this limit our understanding of Chrystal's character?

Later, readers learn that Chrystal has experienced considerable trauma, as her father was almost killed by a lightning strike. She finds it challenging to interact with others her own age and experiences a heightened sensitivity to sounds and textures. She gradually learns to open up to others and share her experience with them in order to build friendships. She also demonstrates some impressive and somewhat unexpected skills, twice saving others on the trek with her knowledge of lightning and her familiarity with the use of a gun.

5 How does this new understanding change your response to Chrystal?

____

____

____

Setting and atmosphere

A Walk in the Dark is set in the Otway Ranges. When the students first arrive to begin their walk, the rainforest is calm and awe-inspiring. As night falls and a storm rolls in, however, it is transformed into a place of danger.

Writers use language to create atmosphere, or an emotional feeling, within the text. Through the careful selection of words, the inclusion of descriptive details and the use of figurative language devices such as **simile** and **metaphor**, writers can shape the emotional responses of their readers – in other words, the mood.

The following two extracts depict the setting of the Otway Ranges at different times in the novel.

simile A device comparing 2 things that are not alike. Similes use 'like', 'as' or 'than' to make the comparison (e.g. The cake was as light as air)
metaphor A type of figurative language used to describe a person or object through an implicit comparison to something with similar characteristics

Extract 1

The bus bounced over the rutted gravel road. Jolted. Revved, skidded a bit on the turns. Finally it came to a stop. There was no sound of the sea, or any other cars or engines. 'You can take your blindfolds off,' said Johan. 'Welcome to the deep, dark wood.' He laughed.

No Australian would describe it like that, thought Elle. For a start, no Australian forest is ever called the wood. That's for gentler forests, in other places, like Holland. Forests of a different scale, where the light is soft and the ground is mossy and feels like thick carpet. Small forests, with pretty trees, delicate leaves. Fields of lilies, poppies, violets. In Australian forests, the gum leaves are tough and don't rot on the ground. The trees shed bark and hard, sharp gumnuts. And you don't see gum trees lining avenues in cities, even Australian cities. Too rough, too asymmetrical, too big, too wild. Still, sometimes when she was running in the forest and allowed herself to stop still for a minute, it reminded Elle of being in a cathedral, like Notre Dame, or that one in Copenhagen. Grundtvig's Church. Which was strange because a cathedral is so ordered, so obviously a built structure. Yet the forest sometimes gave Elle the same feeling of being filled up with something she couldn't explain.

Everyone poured out and around to the side of the bus to get their packs. They were in a clearing, with towering trees overhead. Ash could smell eucalyptus – the messmate and the mountain ash. It was quiet except for the call of currawongs.

7.4 Check for understanding

1 In your own words, describe the setting of the forest at this point in the novel.

2 Highlight in one colour the words in the extract that suggest the wild and untamed nature of the Australian bush.

3 How does the repetition of the word 'too' contribute to this description?

4 Highlight in another colour the references to sensory details: sight, sound, smell and touch.

5 Why do you think Jane Godwin uses these sensory details to help describe the setting?

6 What atmosphere is created by comparing the forest to a cathedral or church?

7 A church is a place that people might go to feel part of a community of people who share the same values, to belong to a world that seems ordered, and to learn lessons about how to live their lives. Why is this an appropriate analogy (parallel or comparison) for how the forest will function for the characters?

Extract 2

A clap, boom. Chrystal dropped Snoopy. 'We need to shelter.'

A blast of wind. Rain pelted down, around.

Wind whirled overhead, bark fell from the sky.

Suddenly, a vibrating roar.

Chrystal started to run. Instinctively, Elle threw back her outstretched arms to protect her. 'STOP!'

A crack like a gunshot.

A crash, something snapping. A wild whoosh of air.

They could feel it under their feet. A tremor in the earth.

A tree was coming down.

The shock went through them, hit the soles of their feet. Jolted them. Elle was trembling. Ash could feel that something, a branch, had scraped his face, it stung and he could sense warm blood filling the scratch. Another flash of light lit the clearing. The tree had crashed into the ground in front of them, its giant stump violently opened, torn and twisted like ripped flesh, white bone. It had brought down other trees with it. Bits were still falling. Elle saw Ash's face, like a strobe light. The deep scratch ran down his cheek. Branches, trees swirled wildly, silver rain slid sideways. Lightning cracked and the whole gully lit up. Massive sound surrounded them. Another bolt of lightning, Elle raced towards the hollow base of a tree. 'In here!' she yelled above the surging storm.

7.5 Check for understanding

1 How would you describe the atmosphere in this extract? Write down three words or phrases.

____

2 Highlight in one colour all the words and phrases that suggest danger or threat.

3 Highlight in another colour all the **verbs** that create a sense of the violence of the storm.

4 This extract makes use of sentence fragments (grammatically incomplete sentences) and very short paragraphs. How do these help to increase the pace and tension of the passage?

____

____

verb A word class that expresses processes that include doing, feeling, thinking, saying and relating

5 How does this depiction of the setting differ from the one in Extract 1? Compare the atmospheres in the two passages, supporting your answer with evidence from the text.

____

____

____

____

6 How does the setting in Extract 2 make you feel? What mood is established?

____

____

Narrative structure

Many coming-of-age novels follow a formula known as 'the hero's journey'. This archetypal **narrative** structure features a protagonist who experiences three phases:

> **narrative** The selection and sequencing of events or experiences, real or imagined, to tell a story to entertain, engage, inform and extend imagination, typically using an orientation, complication and resolution

- the departure: In the exposition of the novel, the protagonist is thrust from the safety and security of their familiar world into the unknown, sometimes with the aid of a mentor or guide.
- the initiation: The protagonist experiences a series of increasingly challenging trials or obstacles through which they develop new skills and understandings. This corresponds to the rising action of the novel. These trials culminate in a final conflict – the climax – in which the protagonist experiences the symbolic death of their naive former self.
- the return: The protagonist returns to the normal world in the novel's resolution, armed with the gift of new knowledge about themselves, and ready to face life on new terms.

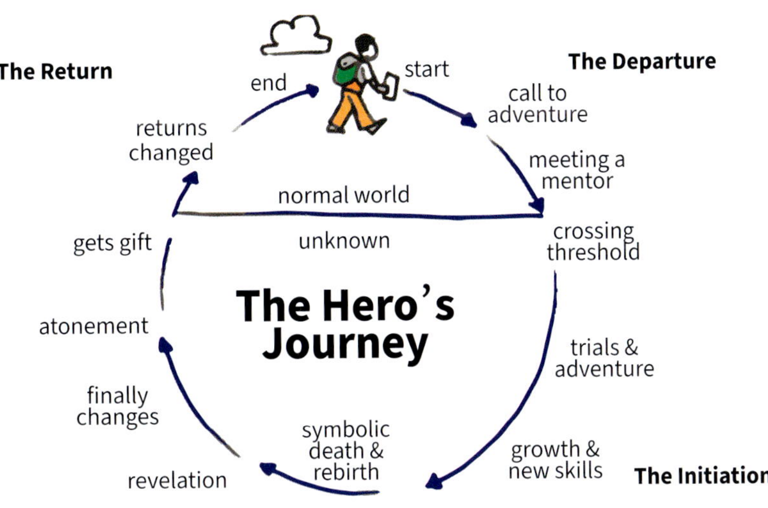

3 What does Ash come to realise about the nature of people as a result of Fred's surprising personal growth?

4 What does this passage suggest is key to developing effective and honest relationships with others?

5 **Symbolism** can be a way to reinforce themes. Why do you think that Jane Godwin chose to set this scene at dawn, following the chaos of the storm during the night?

6 Identify an additional theme explored in the novel. Write a brief paragraph explaining how a character's journey reveals the theme. If you have not read the novel in its entirety, you might identify a typical theme found in coming-of-age novels. Here is an example paragraph.

Understanding social expectations: Ash comes to understand what it means to be a man in today's world. Initially shy, he struggles to stand up to the bullies in the ute who harass the group and label him a girl, but he recognises he must call out Fred's bad behaviour and unwelcome values, such as when Fred criticises Elle's leadership. When Ash realises he is interested in Laila, he is cautious, wondering how he can let her know in a respectful manner. Throughout his journey, he sees how threatening aggressive masculinity can be and how society needs men to be respectful to women and strive for equality.

symbolism The use of one object, person or situation to signify or represent another by giving them meanings that are different from their literal sense (e.g. a dove is a symbol of peace)

7.8 Reflecting and discussing

Discuss the following questions in pairs, in small groups or with the whole class, as directed by your teacher.

1 Do you think *A Walk in the Dark* explores themes typical of the coming-of-age genre?

2 Did the novel conform to your expectations regarding a coming-of-age novel? What did you find interesting or surprising about it?

Developing a personal response

What do we mean by 'a response'?

Our 'response' to a text is our reaction to it. A response to a text includes what we think or feel, or even how our behaviour might change, as a result of our experience of the text. For example, we might admire a character for their resilience or criticise another for their poor attitude. We may consider how a theme is relevant to our own life or even resolve to not make the mistakes made by one of the characters.

We might react to the characters, the themes or the **style** (or way in which the text is written), or we might even react as a result of whether the text meets our expectations. Whenever you consider your response to a text, however, it is important to consider your reaction beyond a simple decision of whether you liked or disliked it.

style The distinctive language features, text structures and/or subject matter in a text which may shape meaning, be enjoyed for its aesthetic qualities or distinguish the work of an author, period etc.

It is important to have a word bank to help explain your responses accurately.

Positive responses	Negative responses
You might find aspects of a text:	*You might find aspects of a text:*
inspiring	confusing
admirable	boring
enlightening	dull
thrilling	predictable
memorable	uninteresting
moving	inconsistent
thought-provoking	repetitive
humorous	slow-paced

7.9

Check for understanding

1 Add five more words to each column in the previous table. You might like to use a thesaurus or search online for words to describe possible responses to a text.

2 Identify three things that *A Walk in the Dark* made you think about. Remember: a personal response is not the same as explaining your understanding of the themes of the text (that is, your interpretation). It is expressing the thoughts that you had in reaction to what you read. For example: *I wondered how I might manage during a night-time trek through the bush, and whether I would be as resilient as the characters were.*

____

____

____

Using evidence

It is also important to use evidence from the text to justify or explain your response. Quoting evidence is an important skill, which you will use many times in your English studies!

» Use quotation marks: When quoting a specific sentence, phrase or section of dialogue from a novel, enclose the quoted text within either single quotation marks (' ') or double quotation marks (" "). Be consistent with the style of quotation marks you choose to use.

» Indicate the speaker or **context**: If you're quoting dialogue, indicate the speaker's name to identify who is speaking. Make sure you provide a simple explanation of the situation you have taken the quote from.

For example: When wondering whether he should kiss Laila, Ash wonders 'if girls trust guys at all anymore'.

context An environment or situation (social, cultural or historical) in which a text is responded to or created. Or wording surrounding an unfamiliar word, which a reader or listener uses to understand its meaning

» Maintain accuracy: When quoting, try to maintain the original wording, punctuation and spelling of the text as closely as possible. However, if you need to make any changes for clarity or to fit the quote into your sentence, use square brackets to indicate any added or modified words or an ellipsis to show that words have been left out. For example, 'Chrystal said, "I am [feeling] better now"' or 'We think we have control ... but some other part of us seems to be working in another way, a way we're not aware of.'

Personal context

The way we respond to a text is often shaped by our personal context. Your 'personal context' refers to the circumstances that surround you and shape who you are. Some of these are listed below.

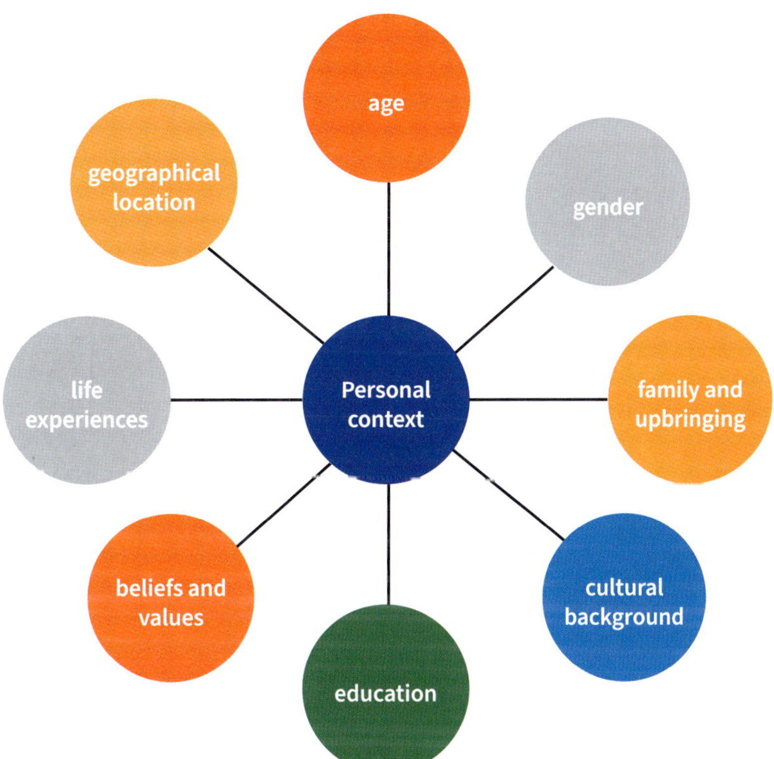

Your personal context can impact your **attitudes** and **values**, your **perspectives** on the world and even the kinds of books and films you like. It influences how you relate to others and navigate challenges and opportunities, as well as your sense of your own identity. Recognising that we are all individuals with unique sets of influences and experiences helps to explain the diversity of perspectives and responses that a group of people will experience.

> **attitudes** Particular ways of thinking and feeling towards people or things
> **values** Ideas and beliefs specific to individuals and groups
> **perspective** A lens through which the author perceives the world and creates a text, or the lens

Writers of coming-of-age stories hope that their readers will see something of themselves in the characters they read about. While your journey might not be identical to the protagonist's, you might recognise similar concerns, experiences or feelings. As a result, you might feel that their journey somewhat reflects your own, and you might even learn a valuable lesson or two from their experience.

In *A Walk in the Dark*, there are five very different protagonists, which means there are several characters with whom readers might identify. Depending on your personal context, you might find you relate to one character more strongly than others.

7.10

Get creative

1 Write an essay exploring your personal response to one character from *A Walk in the Dark*. Plan your essay before you begin writing, using the table below to help you.

Introduction	Introduce the novel by title and author. Introduce your chosen character, explaining their role in the text. Include a thesis statement that identifies your considered response to the character and why you reacted this way.
Body paragraph 1	Explain your initial impressions of your chosen character. Refer to specific examples to explain their characterisation. Use quotes to support your explanation.
Body paragraph 2	Explain the character's growth and the new qualities they develop. Refer to specific examples and use quotes to support your explanation.
Body paragraph 3	Explain your final response to the character. Use quotes to support your explanation. Refer to your own context to explain why you do or do not relate to this character and the journey they have been on.
Conclusion	Restate your response to the character. Summarise the key changes to your response after studying the character's development within the novel.

2 After you have completed your draft, proofread and **edit** your work using the following checklist.

a Check your essay structure for overall **cohesion** and to ensure you have a clear introduction, well-structured body paragraphs and a suitable conclusion. Ensure that you have used connective language to indicate the relationship between your points. ☐

b Ensure that your sentences are grammatically correct, express your ideas clearly and flow smoothly. ☐

c Review spelling, punctuation and grammar and correct any errors. ☐

d Evaluate the effectiveness of your language choices, substituting words to improve accuracy and specificity where needed. ☐

e Ensure that all quotes are seamlessly integrated into your sentences and punctuated correctly. ☐

f Evaluate the logic and credibility of your discussion, ensuring that all points are supported with examples and appropriate discussion. ☐

edit To prepare, alter, adapt or refine with attention to grammar, spelling, punctuation and vocabulary
cohesion Grammatical or lexical relationships that bind different parts of a text together and give it unity. It is achieved through devices such as reference, substitution, repetition and text connectives

Memoir: reflecting on the past

A memoir is a form of autobiographical writing that focuses on specific memories and personal experiences of the author. Unlike an autobiography, which covers an entire life, a memoir zooms in on a particular period, event or theme. The term comes from the French word '*mémoire*', which refers to a written account or narrative based on personal experiences or recollections. It highlights the connection between memory and personal narrative, and is a way for an author to share their unique perspective, emotions and insights with readers, offering a glimpse into their personal journey.

In this unit you will learn:

- about the conventions of memoirs
- how writers use language to represent people, places and events
- how to write your own memoir.

Curriculum content

Australian Curriculum content description	Content code
Analyse how representations of people, places, events and concepts reflect contexts.	AC9E9LY01
Analyse and evaluate how language features are used to represent a perspective of an issue, event, situation, individual or group.	AC9E9LY03
Use comprehension strategies such as visualising, predicting, connecting, summarising, monitoring, questioning and inferring to compare and contrast ideas and opinions in and between texts.	AC9E9LY05
Plan, create, edit and publish written and multimodal texts, organising, expanding and developing ideas, and selecting text structures, language features, literary devices and multimodal features for purposes and audiences in ways that may be imaginative, reflective, informative, persuasive, analytical and/or critical.	AC9E9LY06

Why do people write memoirs?

People write about their lives for a range of reasons. They may have had an interesting or unique life, they may have learned a valuable lesson that they think should be shared with others, or they may be using the writing process as a powerful form of self-expression, helping them to make sense of their own experiences.

The following extracts come from a short memoir titled 'Hippotherapy' from the collection *Growing Up Disabled in Australia*. Written by Alistair Baldwin, a Melbourne-based writer, comedian and director, 'Hippotherapy' recalls his childhood experiences of horse-riding as a therapy intended to assist with his muscular dystrophy.

Whenever I meet someone else who grew up disabled in Australia, there's only one key thing I want to know about them. I go through the small-talk motions, I feign interest in how their day went, I wait a respectful amount of time before I derail the conversation with the question I've been dying to ask.

'Hey, did you have to ride horses too?'

It is one of life's great tragedies that 'hippotherapy' has nothing to do with hippos. Had I, at age eight, received hippo-riding lessons, I think I would have grown up to become a very different man. More confident. More self-assured. Khaki would probably feature more prominently in my wardrobe.

The boring reality is that hippos have to do with horses (hippopotamus derives from the Ancient Greek word for 'river horse'), and it's horses that have to do with hippotherapy.

When it comes to treatment options for a young boy with a congenital muscle disease, one's mind doesn't instinctively jump to horses. Yet therapeutic horse-riding, or hippotherapy, got an emphatic tick of approval from my neurologist, my physio and my occupational therapist.

Such is its popularity that in every state and territory of Australia you can find Riding for the Disabled Association (RDA) centres – made moderately affordable to non-aristocratic disableds through government subsidies. Owing to both ubiquity and these subsidies, I've found that Australian adults with a disability are nearly as likely to have grown up horse-riding as Australian adults who were child actors on

The Saddle Club. Which is to say, quite likely.

My local centre in Perth was called RDA Capricorn. Its stables and paddock were located next to Perry Lakes Stadium, the multipurpose sports complex specially built for the 1962 Commonwealth Games. It was a somewhat ironic neighbour. Perry Lakes was where my able-bodied classmates played basketball, where inter-school athletics carnivals I couldn't compete in were held. I doubt many people knew that within limping distance, hidden among eucalyptus trees and down a discreet dirt road, was a bunch of adolescent cripples on horses.

…

In my first year or so, I always rode Albert. He was an old pony, relatively low to the ground, white with mottled grey specks. Later, as I gained confidence and skill, I rode Apollo – a proper horse, much taller and more muscular, with a chestnut coat.

In each session we would ride around the rectangular paddock a couple times, then crisscross from corner to corner, weave in and out of traffic cones and jump over small obstacles.

There was something exhilarating about turning your steed with the slightest pull of the reins, nailing a jump, shifting gears into a fast trot. What I enjoyed most was the sheer novelty of it. I was, finally, in control of an able body.

8.1 Check for understanding

1 Use a dictionary or the internet to find out the meanings of the following words and write them in the spaces provided.

a feign: ____________________

b congenital: ____________________

c subsidies: ____________________

d ubiquity: ____________________

e ironic: ____________________

f discreet: ____________________

2 Use the internet to research the effects of muscular dystrophy. What does it do to a person's body?

____

____

3 Why does Alistair Baldwin suggest that 'one's mind doesn't instinctively jump to horses' when considering treatment options for people with physical disability

____

____

4 What is implied by the fact that Baldwin says he *might* have grown up differently and been more self-confident and assured? What does this tell you about the kind of person he actually grew up to be?

____

____

5 Why did Baldwin enjoy horse-riding so much? Include evidence from the text to support your answer.

____

____

6 The horse-riding centre is 'hidden among eucalyptus trees and down a discreet dirt road'. What does this suggest about how Baldwin feels society treats disabled people?

____

____

7 Why do you think Baldwin is 'dying to ask' other disabled people if they experienced hippotherapy?

____

____

8 What evidence is there that this memoir is written from the **perspective** of an adult looking back on a childhood experience?

____

____

perspective A lens through which the author perceives the world and creates a text, or the lens through which the reader or viewer perceives the world and understands a text

8.2 Reflecting and discussing

Discuss the following questions in pairs, in small groups or with the whole class as directed by your teacher.

1 Have you or others in your group read any memoirs? If so, who and what were they about? Did you enjoy reading them?

2 Autobiographies, biographies and memoirs are often very popular books that sell in large numbers. Why do you think people are curious to read about other people's lives and experiences?

3 'Hippotherapy' explores the experience of a disabled person. Do you think society is particularly inclusive when it comes to the physically disabled? What challenges do disabled or differently abled people face in contrast to able-bodied people?

Understanding tone

Tone refers to the writer's attitude towards their subject matter. As a memoir is concerned with interpreting past events or experiences, the tone is frequently reflective. However, this will be shaped by other emotional qualities, depending on how the writer feels about the experiences they are sharing. The tone will not necessarily remain constant throughout a memoir, either. As the writer explores their experience, they (and the reader) may experience a rollercoaster of emotions.

Tone is evident in a writer's use of language. To identify tone, consider:

- the word choices made by the author, thinking about their connotations (implied or associated meanings)
- the register, or degree of formality, in the writing
- the details that are focused on, which can suggest what is most important to the writer
- the use of **imagery** and figurative language, which can provide clues about the author's attitude
- the types and structures of sentences used.

tone The mood created by the language features used by an author and the way the text makes the reader feel
imagery Visually descriptive or figurative language to represent things including objects, actions and ideas in ways that appeal to the senses of the reader or viewer

Read this description of the tone in the previous extract from 'Hippotherapy'.

Alistair Baldwin's tone is lighthearted and playful, as he expresses his curiosity about other people's experiences and his whimsical desire for hippo-riding instead of therapeutic horse-riding. There is a sense of wistfulness as he reflects on his childhood experiences and the juxtaposition of his disability with the able-bodied world. The tone becomes excited and empowered when Baldwin describes the joy and novelty of being in control of his movement while riding the horses. Overall, the tone combines wry humour and reflection with a touch of longing.

8.3

Check for understanding

1 Use a dictionary or the internet to find out the meanings of the following words and write them in the spaces below.

a whimsical: ______

b wistful: ______

c wry humour: ______

2 Do you agree with this writer's assessment of the tone? Explain your reasoning.

______

______

______

3 Use a highlighter to identify evidence in the extract from 'Hippotherapy' for each of the tonal qualities below. Label each example. You might use different colours for the different tonal qualities.

For example, one instance of the lighthearted and playful tone is this humorous and hyperbolic (deliberately exaggerated) sentence: 'It is one of life's great tragedies that "hippotherapy" has nothing to do with hippos'.

lighthearted and playful | wistful | excited and empowered

wryly humorous | reflective

Representing experience

It is important to remember that a memoir is a *subjective* representation of someone's experience. This means it is influenced by the writer's personal beliefs, biases and emotions, as well as the quality of their memory, rather than based on objective facts. Memoirs can incorporate elements of fiction, too, recreating dialogue and shaping details in particular ways to improve the **narrative** quality of the story.

When you read a memoir, think carefully about the details that the writer, who is also the subject (protagonist) of the memoir, chooses to share and how they represent or depict their experiences. This

narrative The selection and sequencing of events or experiences, real or imagined, to tell a story to entertain, engage, inform and extend imagination, typically using an orientation, complication and resolution information may be directly stated to the reader, or it may be implied by their responses to events and people; it can also be revealed in the nature of the language they use to describe their experiences.

In this second extract, Alistair Baldwin recalls how his hippotherapy days came to an abrupt end in, as he puts it, 'an event as traumatic as it was bizarre'.

In 2006, a three-year trial of daylight savings began, so that people could try it on for size before buying it for good. The event that led me to quit horse-riding happened a week after we all, sceptically, put our clocks one hour back.

I had my afternoon session as usual. Everyone got the memo and arrived on time. It was a nice, peaceful day. Then, halfway through, we all heard it.

Click. Hissss ...

The Perry Lakes Stadium grounds that the paddock bordered relied on an automatic sprinkler system – those powerful, pressurised ones that always seem to pop out of the ground just as you've laid down your picnic blanket. The system was scheduled to come on at 5.30 p.m., partly so the sun didn't instantly evaporate the water as it sprayed out, and partly because Perry Lakes had been informed that these powerful jets of water spooked the RDA horses, so it was best they didn't go off during a hippotherapy session. But unfortunately, Perry Lakes had not received the daylight savings memo.

Time slowed down. In the millisecond after the click-hiss, Apollo got sucker-punched in the face with water. Before I realised what was happening, I was halfway across the paddock.

Riding horses have four main gaits, ascending in speed like gears in a car. At RDA we only used two: 'walk' and 'trot'. 'Canter', graceful and smooth as it is, was above our abilities. When the sprinklers went off that day, every single horse instinctively shifted into their fourth gear: 'gallop', a gait you may recognise from watching a horse race. In an instant, a dozen tiny, disabled children were flung into the atmosphere.

Apollo's speed suddenly threw me back into the saddle, my spine slamming onto his rump. One leg began waving in the wind like a flag as he charged from one end of the paddock to the other. The other foot remained in the stirrup, and my hands somehow kept hold of the reins.

Apollo was making a dash for the paddock gate, which was shut during sessions, and it was his graceful, speedy jump over it that finally dislodged me from the saddle and sent me down into the mulch with a thud. I fractured two ribs, and couldn't attend the school excursion to the movies the next day.

8.4

Check for understanding

1 Alistair Baldwin himself describes this experience as 'traumatic' and 'bizarre'. Use a highlighter to identify evidence that his accident was traumatic. Use a different-coloured highlighter to identify evidence that it was bizarre.

2 List three other words you might use to describe how Baldwin represents or depicts this experience.

____

3 Do you think that Baldwin has depicted this experience purely objectively (without bias), or do you think some details have been shaped for dramatic effect? Explain your reasoning with examples from the text.

____

____

____

4 Despite the seriousness of this situation, Baldwin still writes about it somewhat humorously. One way in which humour is created is through the absurdity of the daylight savings trial ultimately causing him to be thrown from his horse. Using evidence from the extract, explain three other ways in which humour is generated in this passage.

____

____

____

____

5 Why do you think Baldwin uses humour to write about serious topics such as his disability and a potentially tragic accident?

____

____

Conventions of memoirs

While memoirs can vary considerably in **style**, from conversational recollections of the past to quite formal, essay-like reflections on human experience, there are a number of **conventions** that they usually have in common. These are shown in the following diagram.

style The distinctive language features, text structures and/or subject matter in a text which may shape meaning, be enjoyed for its aesthetic qualities or distinguish the work of an author, period etc.
convention An accepted practice that has developed over time and is generally used and understood (e.g. use of punctuation)
voice The distinct personality of a piece of writing; the individual writing style of the composer, created through the way they use and mix various language features (e.g. a narrative using a child's voice)

In this final extract, Alistair Baldwin moves from simply recollecting a childhood event to reflecting on the significance of his hippotherapy experience and the insights it gave him into his own identity as a disabled person and the nature of disability itself.

Despite their unfortunate and abrupt end, I look back on my horse-riding days with fondness.

Even now, I feel a strange affinity for horses. Partly because of the afternoons I spent with them as a child, and partly because, as with humans, a horse's value to society is inextricably, albeit unfortunately, linked to its abledness. It doesn't take much more than a vague grasp of history and a little imagination to see that, if they could, abled people would melt the lame down into glue.

Beyond that, I'm just glad I was lucky enough to grow up doing something, anything, surrounded by other disabled kids. 'Sail-ability' was a popular kid's maritime activity recommended by my occupational therapists, as was Surfing for the Disabled.

In another life, I'd be writing a charming short story about how daylight savings set off a sequence of events that nearly led to me drowning at sea.

At school, all my friends were abled (as were my enemies). I put so much effort into trying to hide the gap between our abilities. In horse-riding, I never had to disguise the odd way my shoulders rounded, my strange gait, the weird way my hands grasped things. It's exhausting to fight the way you naturally exist. The spaces and moments in which you can relax into how your body truly is are sacred. And that's what horse-riding gave me.

8.5

Check for understanding

1 Do you think the use of first-person **point of view** makes a memoir seem more credible or truthful than a third-person point of view? Give reasons for your answer.

2 The tone in this passage shifts away from the humorous recollection of a childhood event to a more serious and thoughtful reflection on disability. Examine the following quotations carefully. What do they reveal about Baldwin's attitudes and emotions?

a '… as with humans, a horse's value to society is inextricably, albeit unfortunately, linked to its abledness.'

b 'I'm just glad I was lucky enough to grow up doing something, anything, surrounded by other disabled kids.'

c 'I put so much effort into trying to hide the gap between our abilities.'

d 'The spaces and moments in which you can relax into how your body truly is are sacred. And that's what horse-riding gave me.'

3 Complete the following table, drawing on all three extracts from 'Hippotherapy', to summarise what we learn about the subject of this memoir, Alistair Baldwin.

	What we learn about the subject	Evidence from the text
description (background, gender, age, interests etc.)		
three words to describe Alistair Baldwin as a young person		
three words to describe Alistair Baldwin as an adult		

4 A fictional narrative traditionally has an exposition that sets the scene, an escalating series of conflicts for the **protagonist** to face, a climax in which they are most at risk of failure and a resolution that reveals what the protagonist has learned by overcoming their challenges. Baldwin's narrative is non-fiction, but do you think it follows the same structure? Support your response with evidence from the extracts.

point of view The position from which the text is designed to be perceived (e.g. a narrator might take a role of first or third person, omniscient or restricted in knowledge of events or the opinion presented in a text)
protagonist The main character in a text

5 Highlight the phrases in Baldwin's memoir that mark the passing of time or the order of events. Generally, where are they situated in each paragraph? How might this help readers to follow the transitions between past and present?

6 An important aspect of memoir is that it reflects on the significance of the events that the writer recounts. What lessons did Baldwin learn? Support each answer with evidence from the final extract.

a What did Baldwin learn about himself?

b What did Baldwin learn about how disability is viewed in society?

7 Why do you think that, despite his challenges, Baldwin still looks back on this experience 'with fondness'?

8 Most of Baldwin's **audience** is likely to be able-bodied. What do you think he wants readers to appreciate about the experience of disabled people? Is he seeking sympathy or some other reaction from his audience?

audience An intended or assumed group of readers, listeners or viewers that a writer, designer, filmmaker or speaker is addressing

8.6 Get creative

Write a short memoir

tense The form a verb takes to signal the location of a clause in time (e.g. present tense 'has' in 'Jo has a cat' locates the situation in the present; past tense 'had' in 'Jo had a cat' locates it in the past)

Think of a moment in your life that has taught you an important, necessary and serious lesson. Write and publish a short memoir of approximately 800 words to explore the lesson you learned and how you did so.

Write in the first person, use past **tense**, and include details of how you felt and what you thought at the time. Consider, too, what you think and feel today as you look back on this experience.

Your timeline might be chronological, but, depending on the length of time involved, you may need to write a short series of episodes rather than the whole story from beginning to end. Think about how you could use connective language (or transition markers) to indicate the passage of time.

Make sure you think about how you will represent this experience to others. What do you want to communicate about this experience? What do you want your readers to learn or appreciate? Think about the tone you will use, and how you might select language and shape the details of your memoir so that readers will respond in the way you want them to.

Plan your memoir using the table below.

What information is important for the exposition (beginning) of your memoir? Consider time, place, situation and details of your life and self at this point in time.	
What conflict or experience did you face and why was it significant to you then?	
How did you overcome (or not overcome) the conflict?	
What did you learn about yourself or the world as a result?	
How did this experience shape the person you are today?	
What do you want readers to take away from reading about your experience?	

Once you have written your memoir, put together a podcast or a short video based on it. A video could perhaps include some of your own photos. A podcast could be in interview form, which may mean that you need to enlist a classmate to be the interviewer. Present your podcast or video to your class or another intended audience.

UNIT 9

Understanding symbols

A symbol is something that represents a concept or an idea. Some symbols are widely recognised and have specific meanings. Others mean different things to different people or have different meanings depending on when, where and how they are used— in other words, depending on their context. We interpret symbols every day: when obeying traffic signals, selecting apps via the icons on our devices or recognising the logos associated with our favourite brands and organisations. Symbols are also found in art, literature and popular culture, enriching various artworks and other types of communication with layers of meaning. Learning to recognise symbols can help us to engage with the world in a more thoughtful and perceptive manner.

In this unit you will learn:

- how symbols work to represent larger meanings
- how symbols are constructed in visual and written texts.

Curriculum content

Australian Curriculum content description	Content code
Analyse how symbols in still and moving images augment meaning.	AC9E9LA07
Analyse the effect of text structures, language features and literary devices such as extended metaphor, metonymy, allegory, symbolism and intertextual references.	AC9E9LE05
Analyse how representations of people, places, events and concepts reflect contexts.	AC9E9LY01

The Australian National Flag as a symbol

A country's flag is an example of a symbol. It's a symbol that represents the country's identity and serves to foster a sense of unity and belonging among its citizens. The elements of a flag carry meanings that are symbolic of a nation's culture, history and **values**.

The design of the current Australian flag is credited to Ivor Evans, a 14-year-old student from Melbourne, whose design was submitted as part of a competition to create a flag that represented the newly federated country more than a century ago. It was adapted by a panel of judges and officially adopted in 1901.

values Ideas and beliefs specific to individuals and groups

9.1 Reflecting and discussing

Discuss the following questions in pairs, in small groups or with the whole class, as directed by your teacher.

1 Brainstorm places and occasions where the Australian flag is flown. What meaning does the flag have in these **contexts**?

2 What does the Australian flag symbolise to you?

3 The question of whether the current Australian flag represents all Australians is an ongoing issue. Why do some people support a change to the Australian flag?

context An environment or situation (social, cultural or historical) in which a text is responded to or created. Or wording surrounding an unfamiliar word, which a reader or listener uses to understand its meaning

9.2 Check for understanding

1 Add the correct letter to each box beside the Australian flag below to label the elements listed underneath it. You may need to do some research first.

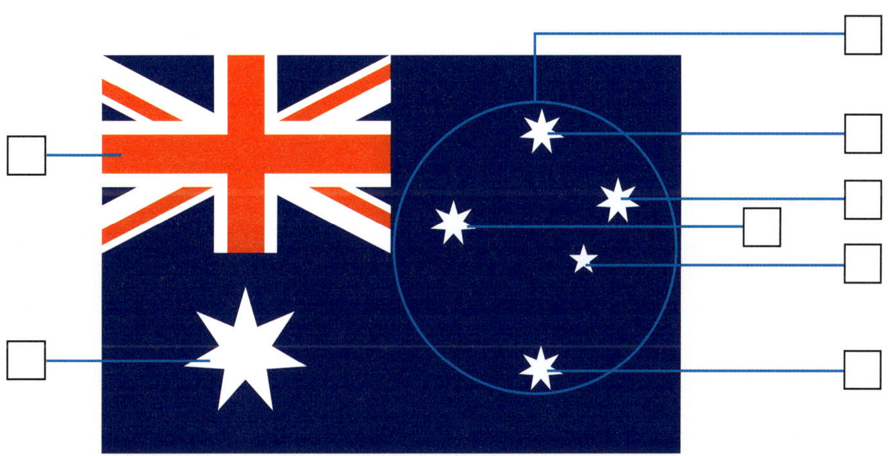

a Union Jack

b Commonwealth Star

c Alpha Crucis

d Beta Crucis

e Delta Crucis

f Epsilon Crucis

g Gamma Crucis

h Southern Cross constellation as a whole

2 What does each of the following major elements of the Australian flag symbolise to you?

a Union Jack: ____________________

b Commonwealth Star: ____________________

c Southern Cross: ____________________

3 What is the significance of the seven points on the Commonwealth Star?

____

4 The four principal stars of the Southern Cross are said to represent the four moral virtues of justice, prudence, temperance and fortitude. What do these terms mean?

a justice: ____________________

b prudence: ____________________

c temperance: ____________________

d fortitude: ____________________

5 Do you think these are qualities that should be upheld by Australians? Explain your answer.

____

____

6 What do the colours of the Australian flag express about our national identity? Do these colours tie us closely to the flags of any other nations?

____

____

Look closely at the following photographs. National flags are used on many occasions and in a variety of situations in which they have particular purposes and symbolic meanings.

Citizenship ceremony

Protest march

Sporting occasion

Australian Defence Force

9.3 Check for understanding

Complete the table below by answering the questions in relation to each of the previous images.

Images	For what purpose is the flag being used?	What might the flag mean to this group of people?	How might their context influence the meaning they associate with the flag?
citizenship ceremony			
Australian Defence Force			
sporting occasion			
protest march			

The Australian Aboriginal Flag and the Torres Strait Islander Flag

Since 1995, the Australian Aboriginal Flag and the Torres Strait Islander Flag have been considered official flags of Australia and flown alongside the Australian National Flag. They are important symbols recognising Australia's First Nations peoples.

9.4 Check for understanding

1 Visit the website of the Department of the Prime Minister and Cabinet to find out the origins and meanings of these flags. Annotate each flag, identifying the various symbols, including the colour choices, that make up the design.

2 While you are there, you might like to investigate the various other official flags that are used to represent Australia in different contexts, such as the Red Ensign.

Changing the Australian National Flag

There have been many debates about whether we need a more suitable flag to reflect a more independent and multicultural Australia. While some people argue that the flag needs to change to reflect our current context, others disagree. Read the comments below.

'I'm very supportive of a new flag. We have so much more to represent than just the mother country, a constellation and the states. And make it green and gold!'

'Yes, we definitely need a new flag. Seinfeld described our flag as "Britain by night" – a very witty and telling description. We need a flag that represents modern Australia that has all but cut her links with Britain and is an independent and multicultural nation, not some British colony.'

'I strongly support retention of our current national flag because it shows where we are (Southern Cross), governance arrangement (Commonwealth Star), and the source of our democracy, language, rule of law, freedom of speech, and respect for all individuals (Union Jack). It is the most beautiful of all national flags.'

'Let's keep our national flag as it is and be proud of it. Our parents and grandparents fought and died for this flag and the freedom it represents. It is a flag that is respected worldwide, and the majority of people know who it belongs to. Keep the pride alive.'

There have been many attempts to design a new national flag, such as this one designed by John Blaxland with Sancho Murphy.

The colours combine those of the Australian National Flag and the Australian Aboriginal Flag, with the boomerang as both a symbol of First Nations culture and suggestive of a fragment from the Union Jack. The dots within the Commonwealth Star represent the hundreds of Aboriginal, Torres Strait Islander and migrant languages within our multicultural nation. Combined in this way, the design is intended to reflect values of inclusivity, multiculturalism and reconciliation, as well as our national identity.

9.5 Get creative

Design your own Australian flag. As you plan your design, consider the following questions.

1 What values do you see as important for modern Australia?

2 What aspects of national identity do you think the flag should communicate?

3 What symbols do you think might represent these ideas?

Draw your design in the space below, annotating the symbols you have used.

You might like to research some of the other designs that have been suggested to replace the Australian National Flag and compare them with your own design.

Everyday symbols

There are many symbols that we use every day as shortcuts for information or concepts. From road traffic signs to images on packaging and icons on our devices, we interpret – sometimes without even thinking – the symbols that surround us.

9.6 Check for understanding

Use the internet to research the meanings and origins of the following symbols.

Symbols	Meanings	Origins

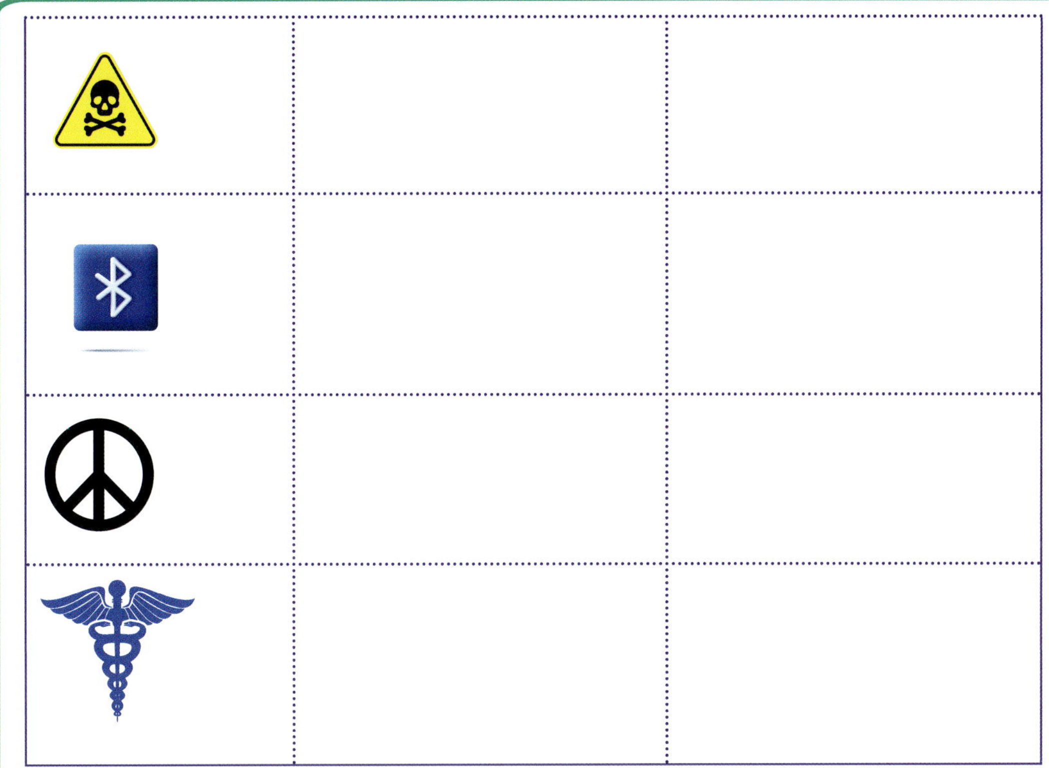

Symbolism in stories

Symbols aren't always communicated in visual form. Authors frequently construct symbols in their writing to suggest ideas, create atmosphere or add layers of meaning to their work. Symbols are a kind of shorthand that save writers from needing to spell everything out to the reader while still creating complexity and depth in their work.

'The Drover's Wife' is a famous short story by Henry Lawson. It describes the challenging experiences of a pioneer woman who fends for herself and her family while her husband is away droving cattle. She battles the harsh weather, a mad bullock and suspicious strangers. The story contains a number of symbols, including a snake that invades the family's rustic home and a dog that helps to protect the family members.

9.7 Check for understanding

Read these short extracts, in which the snake makes its first appearance.

Extract 1

Four ragged, dried-up-looking children are playing about the house. Suddenly one of them yells: 'Snake! Mother, here's a snake!'

The gaunt, sun-browned bushwoman dashes from the kitchen, snatches her baby from the ground, holds it on her left hip, and reaches for a stick.

'Where is it?'

'Here! gone into the wood-heap!' yells the eldest boy – a sharp-faced urchin of eleven. 'Stop there, mother! I'll have him. Stand back! I'll have the beggar!'

'Tommy, come here, or you'll be bit. Come here at once when I tell you, you little wretch!'

The youngster comes reluctantly, carrying a stick bigger than himself. Then he yells, triumphantly:

'There it goes – under the house!' and darts away with club uplifted. At the same time the big, black, yellow-eyed dog-of-all-breeds, who has shown the wildest interest in the proceedings, breaks his chain and rushes after that snake. He is a moment late, however, and his nose reaches the crack in the slabs just as the end of its tail disappears.

Extract 2

An evil pair of small, bright bead-like eyes glisten at one of these holes. The snake – a black one – comes slowly out, about a foot, and moves its head up and down. The dog lies still, and the woman sits as one fascinated. The snake comes out a foot farther. She lifts her stick, and the reptile, as though suddenly aware of danger, sticks his head in through the crack on the other side of the slab, and hurries to get his tail round after him.

1 Find definitions for the following words in the extract.

gaunt: ______________________________

urchin: ______________________________

2 What evidence is there that the snake represents a danger to the family?

____

____

3 What is significant about the fact that the snake invades their home?

____

____

4 Why do you think the snake comes to symbolise the threats faced by the bushwoman?

____

____

5 Snakes symbolise different concepts in different contexts. The Biblical story of Adam and Eve has seen the snake associated with evil and danger, but other cultures have different ideas. Use the internet to find out which cultures see the snake as a symbol of:

a healing and medicine: ______

b renewal and rebirth: ______

c kundalini, a form of healing energy: ______

d eternity or infinity: ______

6 What quality of the snake is recognised in each of these symbolic representations?

______

______

Read this short extract, in which we learn more about the family dog, Alligator, who sits up with the woman while she keeps watch for the snake.

Extract 3

It must be near one or two o'clock. The fire is burning low. Alligator lies with his head resting on his paws, and watches the wall. He is not a very beautiful dog, and the light shows numerous old wounds where the hair will not grow. He is afraid of nothing on the face of the earth or under it. He will tackle a bullock as readily as he will tackle a flea. He hates all other dogs – except kangaroo-dogs – and has a marked dislike to friends or relations of the family. They seldom call, however.

7 Identify the qualities suggested by the following facts about Alligator.

a He will tackle a bullock as readily as he will tackle a flea. ______

b He is close to his mistress but not anyone outside the family. ______

8 Snakes and dogs are not the only animals that have symbolic meanings. Find out the symbolic meanings associated with the following animals, as well as the origins of these symbolic meanings. The first one has been done for you.

Animals	Symbolic meanings	Origins
owl	wisdom	Owls are associated with the Greek goddess Athena, who was known for her wisdom and foresight.
butterfly		
dove		
lion		
sheep		

Symbolism in poetry

Symbolism is a tool that poets use to represent ideas, feelings or objects beyond their literal meanings. By using symbols like objects, colours or natural elements, poets can create vivid and powerful **imagery** that engages our imagination and helps us connect with the deeper layers of their poems' messages.

symbolism The use of one object, person or situation to signify or represent another by giving them meanings that are different from their literal sense (e.g. a dove is a symbol of peace)
imagery Visually descriptive or figurative language to represent things including objects, actions and ideas in ways that appeal to the senses of the reader or viewer

Loki Liddle is a Jabirr Jabirr man from the Kimberley region in Western Australia. As well as writing poetry, he is a spoken word artist and singer, and therefore knows a thing or two about the power of language! This poem by Loki Liddle is titled 'Angus', and in it the persona reflects on his relationship with his friend who was like a brother, as well as his identity as a First Nations Australian.

Angus

At dawn in the innocent blue waters of Flat Rock
His favourite place on Earth
Years before he taught me to make my first fire
Under the midnight hum of stars.

Revelries, visions, water and sleep.
We came of age in that place
As he put my head on the rock and my heart in sand
And demanded that I feel the pulse of the land

So I did.

And felt a beat from the East Coast to the West
Where my own country Broome was calling me home
But I was found now ... and known.
Years have passed and I still need to go.

But when I sit by the fire I sit there alone
Because his pulse stopped at dawn
in the innocent blue waters of Flat Rock
I am there only to call my Ancestors via landline
To see his face in stars that spiral like vines

It's his heart I hear pulse through the waves
The soul of my brother that will always remain
A phantom shape
In the salt and the spray.

9.8

Check for understanding

1 What do you think this poem is about? Write a sentence or two that capture the main ideas of the poem. You might consider the relationship between the persona and his friend, as well as their connection to Country.

____

____

2 Why do you think the poem begins at dawn? What might this time of day symbolise?

____

____

3 Which lines best symbolise the persona learning about his spiritual connection to Country?

____

____

4 Why do you think Liddle uses the symbolism of waves to represent the heartbeat and soul of his friend?

____

____

Pathetic fallacy

Pathetic fallacy is a type of symbolism in which human emotions are associated with weather or other natural phenomena. This technique is used by authors to create a specific mood, enhance the atmosphere or reflect the emotions of the characters or events in a story. It helps us to connect more deeply with the story and understand the emotions, as they are conveyed in a vivid and imaginative way.

9.9 Check for understanding

Draw lines to matchv the following symbols with the human emotions and experiences they might represent. One has been done for you.

a storm	change or the end of a cycle
autumn leaves falling	sadness or melancholy
dawn	foreboding or a sense of trouble brewing
drizzling rain	chaos or turbulence
dark clouds on the horizon	a sense of hope or rebirth
spring	new beginnings

9.10 Get creative

Write your own poem using symbolism. Use the following steps to help you.

1 Choose a **theme** or emotion that you want to explore in your poem. It could be something like love, loss, freedom or courage. Think about the deeper meaning or message you want to convey.

2 Brainstorm a list of symbols that are associated with your chosen theme or emotion. Symbols can include objects, animals, colours or elements of nature. Think about the qualities or associations connected with each symbol and identify how they can enhance the meaning of your poem.

3 Incorporate your chosen symbols into your poem as you begin writing. Integrate them into the imagery, **metaphors** or descriptions in your poem.

4 Use descriptive language to paint a vivid picture in the reader's mind. Show rather than tell, using sensory details and imagery to bring your symbols to life. Allow your imagination to soar and experiment with creative ways to express your ideas.

theme The main idea, concept or message of a text
metaphor A type of figurative language used to describe a person or object through an implicit comparison to something with similar characteristics

UNIT 10

From Shakespeare to smartphones

From 'thou' in Shakespeare's plays to 'u' in current text messaging, the way we use English has evolved and continues to evolve. We also use different versions of the language at different times. In English classes, you might study the language used by Shakespeare or by other authors from different eras. At home, you might speak a hybrid version of English that mixes English words with words from another language. Among your friends, you may have words or phrases that people outside your group might not understand which have arisen from shared experiences and conversation. Part of being a good communicator is knowing which form of language to use in different situations and contexts.

In this unit you will learn:

- how the English language has evolved over time
- how identity influences language
- how context influences the way in which we communicate with others.

Curriculum content

Australian Curriculum content description	Content code
Recognise how language empowers relationships and roles.	AC9E9LA01
Create and edit literary texts, that may be a hybrid, that experiment with text structures, language features and literary devices for purposes and audiences.	AC9E9LE06
Understand how spelling is used in texts for particular effects; for example, characterisation, humour and to represent accents and distinctive speech.	AC9E9LY08

Romeo and Juliet

Romeo and Juliet by William Shakespeare was written around 1595 and first published in 1597. The so-called balcony scene is one of the most famous scenes in *Romeo and Juliet*. It takes place in Act II, scene ii, when Romeo observes Juliet standing at her window.

AN
EXCELLENT
conceited Tragedie
OF
Romeo and Iuliet,
As it hath been often (with great applause) plaid publiquely, by the right Honourable the L. of Hunsdon his Seruants.

LONDON,
Printed by Iohn Danter.
1597

Interestingly, a 'balcony' does not appear in Shakespeare's play script, and the word itself does not appear in print until 1618. Also interesting is the fact that in the original play, this scene is not a separate scene at all and continues from Act II, scene i. Despite this, the image of Juliet at her balcony has become an enduring one – so much so that a 'Juliet balcony' is the architectural term for any kind of narrow balcony or railing outside a window.

Although recognisably English, the language used in the 1632 Second Folio, or second edition, of Shakespeare's works looks a little different from the language we use today.

But ſoft, what light through yonder window breaks?
It is the Eaſt, and Iuliet is the Sunne.
Ariſe faire Sun and kill the envious Moone,
Who is already ſicke and pale with griefe,
That thou, her Maid, are far more faire than ſhe.

10.1 Reflecting and discussing

Discuss the following questions in pairs, in small groups or with the whole class, as directed by your teacher.

1. What differences do you notice between the English used in this extract and the English we use today?
2. How easy is the text in the extract to read?
3. You might notice that some instances of the letter 's' look different from others. What can you find out about the use of the 'long s' (ſ) in early English texts?

Some writers experiment with language evolution by adapting or transforming **literary texts** into a new form or **style**. The two extracts below are taken from *Romeo and Juliet* by William Shakespeare and *YOLO Juliet* by Brett Wright. The latter is a parody of *Romeo and Juliet* and retells the story in text messages and status updates.

literary text Past and contemporary texts across a range of cultural contexts which are valued for their form and style and are recognised as having artistic value
style The distinctive language features, text structures and/or subject matter in a text which may shape meaning, be enjoyed for its aesthetic qualities or distinguish the work of an author, period etc.

JULIET appears above at a window

ROMEO:

But, soft! What light through yonder window breaks?
It is the east, and Juliet is the sun.
Arise, fair sun, and kill the envious moon,
Who is already sick and pale with grief,
That thou her maid art far more fair than she:
…
It is my lady, O, it is my love!
O, that she knew she were!
…
Two of the fairest stars in all the heaven,
Having some business, do entreat her eyes
To twinkle in their spheres till they return.
What if her eyes were there, they in her head?
The brightness of her cheek would shame those stars,
As daylight doth a lamp; her eyes in heaven
Would through the airy region stream so bright
That birds would sing and think it were not night.
See, how she leans her cheek upon her hand!
O, that I were a glove upon that hand,
That I might touch that cheek!

JULIET:

O Romeo, Romeo! wherefore art thou Romeo?
Deny thy father and refuse thy name;
Or, if thou wilt not, be but sworn my love,
And I'll no longer be a Capulet.
…
'Tis but thy name that is my enemy;
Thou art thyself, though not a Montague.
What's Montague? It is nor hand, nor foot,
Nor arm, nor face, nor any other part
Belonging to a man. O, be some other name!
What's in a name? That which we call a rose
By any other name would smell as sweet;
…
Romeo, doff thy name,
And for thy name, which is no part of thee,
Take all myself.

ROMEO:

I take thee at thy word.
Call me but love, and I'll be new baptised;
Henceforth I never will be Romeo.

[Scene 2]

Romeo has checked into the Grounds Below Juliet's Balcony

Voice Memo from Romeo

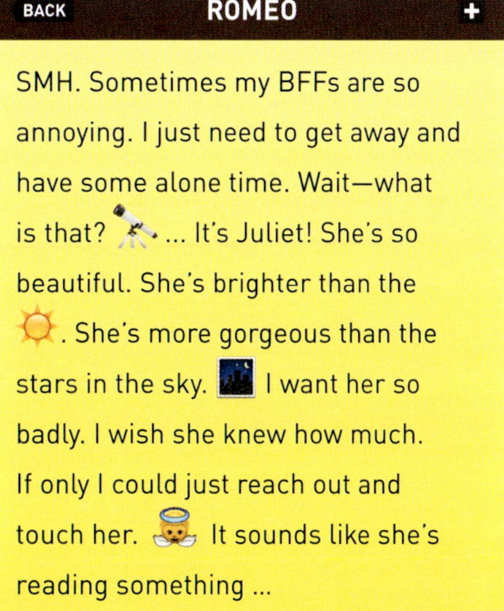

Voice Memo from Juliet

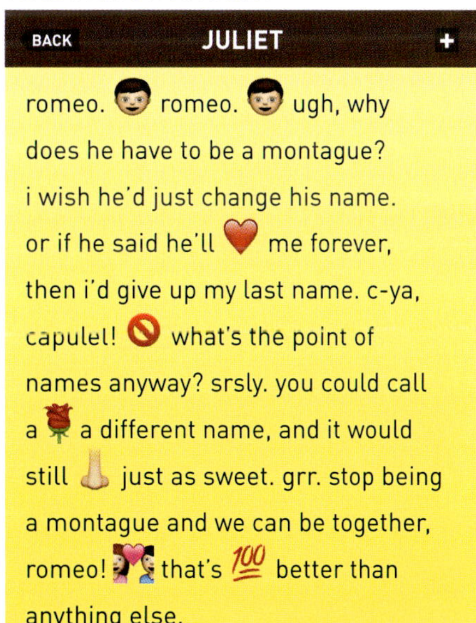

Voice Memo from Romeo

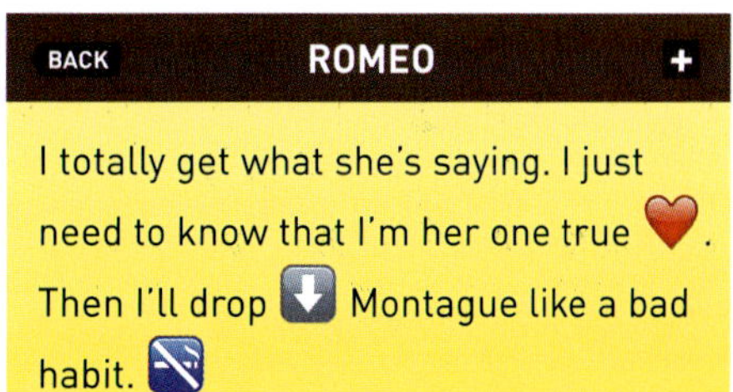

JULIET:
What man art thou that thus bescreened in night
So stumblest on my counsel?
ROMEO:
My name, dear saint, is hateful to myself,
Because it is an enemy to thee;
Had I it written, I would tear the word.
JULIET:
How camest thou hither, tell me, and wherefore?
The orchard walls are high and hard to climb,
And the place death, considering who thou art,
If any of my kinsmen find thee here.
ROMEO:
With love's light wings did I o'er-perch these walls;
For stony limits cannot hold love out,
And what love can do that dares love attempt;
Therefore thy kinsmen are no stop to me.
JULIET:
If they do see thee, they will murder thee.
ROMEO:
I have night's cloak to hide me from their eyes;
And but thou love me, let them find me here.
My life were better ended by their hate,
Than death prorogued, wanting of thy love.

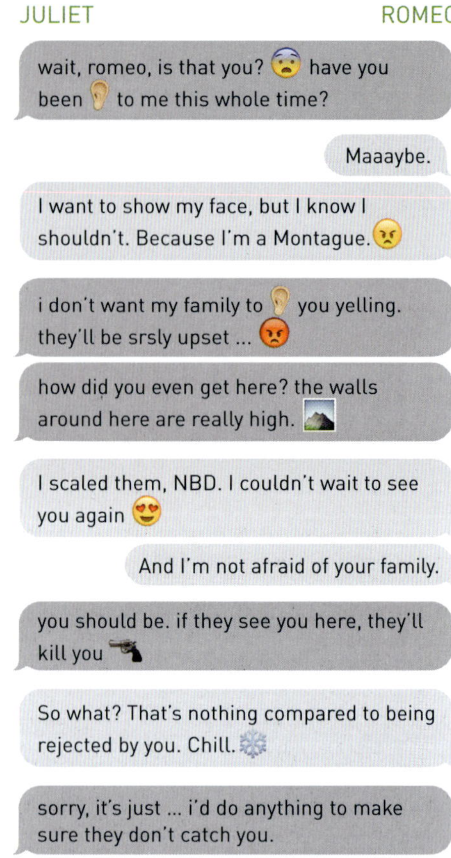

10.2 Check for understanding

1 Look up the definitions for each of the following words from *Romeo and Juliet* and write them in the spaces provided.

a yonder: ______

b entreat: ______

c doff: ______

d prorogued: ______

2 Identify the contemporary words that have replaced the following archaisms (very old-fashioned words).

Archaisms	Contemporary replacements
thou	
doth	
wherefore	

wilt	
thy	
thee	
hither	

3 How does Romeo feel about Juliet? Support your answer with evidence from Shakespeare's text.

4 Why is Juliet concerned about Romeo being part of the Montague family? Support your answer with evidence from Shakespeare's text.

5 Does the language used in *YOLO Juliet* convey Shakespeare's ideas more clearly to you than the language used in the original play? Explain why, using examples from both versions.

6 Does the language used in *YOLO Juliet* (such as abbreviations, emojis and non-standard punctuation) seem natural to you, or does it sound like an adult trying to be 'cool'? Support your answer with examples from the text.

The evolution of English

Old English

English traces its roots back to the Germanic tribes that migrated to Britain in the early medieval period, around the fifth and sixth centuries. These tribes, such as the Angles, Saxons and Jutes, brought their languages, which eventually merged to form what we now call Old English.

Old English looked quite different from modern English, with many additional letters, such as þ and ð (two different versions of 'th'). It also had a complex grammar system and a vocabulary that differed greatly from what we use today. Some words that have remained relatively unchanged since this time include man, woman, child (cild), house (hūs), day (dæg), night (niht), book (bōc), sun (sunne), earth (eorþe), and water (wæter).

Middle English

Interactions with the Vikings and their language of Old Norse greatly impacted Old English, shaping its grammar as well as its vocabulary. Then, in the eleventh century, the Norman Conquest of England took place. The Normans, led by William the Conqueror, brought with them the French language, which influenced the English spoken by the ruling class.

Over time, English began to absorb French words and integrate them into the language. Some of these terms related to the food prepared for the Norman rulers, which is why we raise cows and pigs but eat beef and pork. Other borrowed words from this era include justice, government, majesty, feast, cathedral, palace, honour – all words important to those in power!

Modern English

From the sixteenth century, a lot of change happened. The Renaissance and the Age of Exploration brought new foreign words and **phrases** to English, and the invention of the printing press saw the standardisation of spelling and grammar. The **dialect** used in London, where the printing presses were mostly located, became the norm. The first English dictionary was published in 1604, further contributing to a shared understanding of the English language.

Further changes during the Industrial Revolution saw the invention of many new words, and England's colonies began standardising their own versions of English. Words from this era include electricity, camera, telegraph, train, engine, reservoir and combustion.

Today, new technologies and increasing multiculturalism contribute to the continuing evolution of English.

phrase A group of words often beginning with a preposition but without a subject and verb combination (e.g. 'on the river'; 'with brown eyes')
dialect Form of a language distinguished by features of vocabulary, grammar and pronunciation particular to a region

10.3 Check for understanding

1 Use the internet to find five more words that came from each of these periods of English language development.

Old English	Middle English	Modern English

2 Use the internet to find the meanings and origins of the following words in English that were borrowed from other languages. The first one has been done for you.

Words	Origins	Meanings
anonymous	Greek	something or someone without a name
kindergarten		
safari		
cartoon		
karaoke		
cookie		
lemon		
avatar		
ketchup		
penguin		
koala		

3 Do you think new words make our language more useful and interesting? Explain why or why not.

4 Does the introduction of words from other cultures make us more inclusive (willing to accept differences)? Again, explain why or why not.

5 Words can also disappear from a language. Sometimes, these words have been replaced by words entering from new languages; at other times, they are colloquial (slang) words that just fall out of favour. Two examples are below. Add to the table by researching other 'disappeared' words that deserve a comeback!

Words	Meanings
snollygoster	a clever but unprincipled person; used in the early twentieth century
huckmuck	an Old English word for the confusion that comes when things are not in their proper place

Shakespeare's inventions

Shakespeare loved to experiment with language. He invented words and borrowed from Latin and French. He is credited with introducing more than 1700 new words to the English language, many of which are still used today. He was the first to use such words as bump, dwindle, courtship and lonely. He also joined independent words to make compounds such as love-song and cutthroat, and he invented many expressions, including those in the following table.

10.4 Check for understanding

Fill in the table with the meaning of each expression.

Shakespearean expressions	Plays	Meanings
wild goose chase	*Romeo and Juliet*	
at one fell swoop	*Macbeth*	
method in my madness	*Hamlet*	
in a pickle	*The Tempest*	
green-eyed monster	*Othello*	

The evolution of word order

It is not just individual words that evolve; the way we structure language can develop over time, too. Today, the most common word order in a sentence or **clause** is **subject**—**verb**—object. Consider the clause 'I will bear the light'.

subject	*verb*	*object*
I	will bear	the light

clause A grammatical unit referring to a happening or state e.g. 'the team won' (happening), 'the dog is red' (state), usually containing a subject and a verb group/phrase
subject A word or group of words (usually a noun group/phrase) in a sentence or clause representing the person, thing or idea doing the action that follows (e.g. 'The dog [subject] was barking')
verb A word class that expresses processes that include doing, feeling, thinking, saying and relating

In Shakespeare's time, however, word order was much less standardised. In *Romeo and Juliet*, clauses and sentences commonly appear with an inverted word order. Here are some examples.

'O where is Romeo, *saw you him* today?'

verb	*subject*	*object*
saw	you	him

'His looks I fear

object	*subject*	*verb*
His looks	I	fear

Scholars have suggested that the subject–object–verb structure in particular was more common in the Germanic languages that contributed to Old English. However, most agree that Shakespeare manipulated word order for mostly poetic reasons, to create emphasis and rhythm in his dialogue.

Yoda, a character in the *Star Wars* films, is famously known for structuring his sentences in the object–subject–verb structure – for example, 'Patience you must have' and 'Truly wonderful the mind of a child is'.

10.5

Check for understanding

1 Rewrite these sentences using the subject–verb–object structure.

a The feast they devoured. ______

b She the grammar exercises completed. ______

c A car my dog chased. ______

2 Write three humorous sentences of your own in 'Yoda-speak' – that is, in object–subject–verb order.

______

Portmanteau words

One common way in which new words come about is the blending together of two existing words – for example, 'brunch', meaning a mixture of breakfast and lunch. This kind of word is called a 'portmanteau word'.

10.6

Check for understanding

1 Fill in the table with the original words that were combined to form the following portmanteau words.

Portmanteaus	Original words
webinar	
smog	
bromance	
frenemy	
chillax	
upcycling	
glamping	

2 Writers sometimes create their own portmanteau words to describe unique concepts. Create three portmanteau words of your own to describe experiences you have had.

Portmanteaus	Original words	New meanings

Changing meanings

Sometimes a word doesn't change but its meaning does. Many words today have developed additional meanings due to new uses in the **context** of technology.

context An environment or situation (social, cultural or historical) in which a text is responded to or created. Or wording surrounding an unfamiliar word, which a reader or listener uses to understand its meaning

10.7 Check for understanding

Add definitions to these words to indicate their new meanings in the context of technology use. The first one has been done for you.

Words	Original meanings	New meanings
save	to rescue or retrieve	to record or preserve a document
mouse		
cursor		
loot		
spam		
cookie		
easter egg		

Language evolution and identity

Language also evolves to represent the culture and identity of those who speak it. This can refer to the way English has been adapted by those who have migrated to English-speaking countries or to those who have had English imposed upon them by colonisation.

Aboriginal English

Aboriginal English has its own structure, rules and vocabulary. Like other languages, it also has many regional variations within it, reflecting the richness and diversity of the many First Nations peoples living in Australia. Sometimes Aboriginal English is thought to be poorly spoken English, but this is not the case; rather, it follows its own grammatical rules, even if those rules differ from **Standard Australian English**. It is a complex language that has evolved in response to colonisation, enabling First Nations Australians to operate within the dominant culture while continuing to reflect their cultural identity.

Standard Australian English Recognised as the 'common language' of Australians, it is the dynamic and evolving spoken and written English used for official or public purposes and recorded in dictionaries, style guides and grammars

One way in which this is evident is in relationship terms such as Aunty and Uncle, which in Aboriginal English are used to convey respect to senior people, including those not biologically related to the speaker. As such, the terms reflect First Nations Australians' understandings of kinship (family relations).

Similarly, the concept of 'Country' is broader than traditional English usage, referring to the land to which a First Nations Australian belongs and their place of Dreaming. Aboriginal English includes words from various First Nations languages, such as 'corroboree', which, although an Eora word, is commonly used across the country. Other words you may have heard used include 'deadly' to refer to something great, 'mob' to refer to someone's family or community, and 'yarning' to refer to important conversations.

While it is important to know about Aboriginal English, it is not considered appropriate for people who are not First Nations Australians to use it. This is because it reflects unique cultural identities of First Nations peoples.

Subcultures

Language can also evolve to represent the identities of particular subcultures or social groups, based on occupations or interests. Gamers, for example, have a whole range of slang, **jargon**, acronyms and **idioms** that might be virtually unintelligible to those who are outside that culture. These include 'GG' (good game), 'noob' (newbie, a novice player) and 'pwned' (used to express superiority).

jargon Technical words specific to a certain group, such as medical or legal jargon
idiom An expression whose meaning does not relate to the literal meaning of its words (e.g. 'They went out to paint the town red')

Subcultures can develop their own unique forms of communication. The specific languages associated with subcultures are used to:

- communicate effectively with others in the group
- establish a sense of belonging, while excluding outsiders
- convey a creative expression of identity.

10.8 Reflecting and discussing

Discuss the following questions in pairs, in small groups or with the whole class, as directed by your teacher.

1. What words and phrases do you and your friends use that might not be understood by others, such as your teachers or other adults?
2. Where do these terms come from? How have they evolved?
3. Do you feel that using language in this way is designed to exclude adults and children? That is, is it about expressing a uniquely teenage identity?
4. Do you or others in your group identify as part of a subculture that has its own unique language? Is that language an important part of its members' identity?

10.9 Get creative

1 Experiment with language to transform a text. Select a text written in Standard Australian English that you know well and rewrite it using non-standard English. A poem, short story or short extract from a novel would work well as the basis for your adaptation.

2 You can choose to write a humorous parody of the original text in which you adapt the text for a new audience, such as today's teenagers. Experiment with words, sentence structure and spelling, using at least three of the following:

neologisms (newly invented words) sentence fragments

non-standard spelling slang jargon emojis

3 Your use of non-standard English should be purposeful; that is, the ideas in your chosen text should be clear to the reader, and you must have good reasons for experimenting with language in the ways that you do.

Translate Shakespeare into 'Aussie'. Choose a scene from *Romeo and Juliet*. You can easily find complete versions of the play online – some with modern English translations. Adapt the scene using Australian slang. There are several Australian slang dictionaries online that might help you, such as the Australian Word Map, but choose words carefully to make sure that your final piece is appropriate for your classroom context.

Consider every aspect of the text in your transformation; for example, you might give the characters typical Aussie nicknames, such as Rozza and Jules, and set the scene at a barbecue or after a school formal.

Using comprehension strategies

Every day, you will come across a range of texts that you need to comprehend. To 'comprehend' something means to understand and make meaning from it. These texts that you are required to understand might include an advertisement on television, a recipe for dinner, a train timetable, an explanation in a textbook, a webpage, a chapter of a novel, or the feed on a social media site. Clearly, comprehension plays a vital role in all of our lives on a daily basis. Well-developed comprehension skills allow us to function easily rather than living in a state of complete confusion.

In this unit you will learn:

- about different comprehension strategies
- to use comprehension strategies for a range of text forms
- to use comprehension strategies to enhance your understanding and enjoyment of texts.

Curriculum content

Australian Curriculum content description	Content code
Analyse how representations of people, places, events and concepts reflect contexts.	AC9E9LY01
Use comprehension strategies such as visualising, predicting, connecting, summarising, monitoring, questioning and inferring to compare and contrast ideas and opinions in and between texts.	AC9E9LY05

What are comprehension strategies?

comprehension strategies Processes used by readers to make meaning from texts. They include activating and using prior knowledge, predicting likely future events in a text, monitoring meaning and critically reflecting

Comprehension strategies are the specific processes we use to make sense of texts so that we can understand them. This unit will particularly draw your attention to the following comprehension skills:

Each of these strategies is explained separately below. However, it is important to remember that often you will use more than one strategy at the same time to comprehend a text. Indeed, the Check for understanding and Reflecting and discussing activities throughout Units 1–10 of this book integrate a range of different comprehension strategies simultaneously.

In this unit, the comprehension strategies that are a particular focus in each section are indicated before the activities commence. This will help you to be aware of the specific processes you are using in each activity.

Summary of common comprehension strategies

Skimming is reading quickly in order to get a general overview of a text. It only allows for an overall impression of the text but is a very useful strategy in helping you decide what kind of text you are reading and identifying its main topic.

Scanning involves reading quickly in order to find specific facts, words or phrases. This strategy requires you to move your eyes quickly down the text to find only the information that will answer a particular question.

Activating prior knowledge requires you to think about what you already know to help you understand a new text. It may involve brainstorming what you already know about a text's main topic or making connections with something similar you have already read.

Visualising involves forming a mental image or picture in your head to illustrate what you are reading.

Predicting involves making a logical presumption about what might happen next in a text, often based on prior experience of similar texts.

Connecting is about making links between the text you are trying to understand and other texts. It also involves thinking about how the text relates to you and to the world at large.

Summarising involves choosing only the most important information in a text and then rewriting it in shortened form.

Questioning refers to asking yourself questions before, during or after reading a text, in ways that help you think more deeply about what you are reading and help clarify your understanding.

Inferring means making a deduction about what something might mean. Even though a text might not state something specifically, you will be able to draw logical conclusions based on the clues or hints it offers and through your skills of reasoning.

Comprehension focus 1: scanning, summarising and inferring

The following text is a work of flash fiction written by Richard Holt.

A Royal Kiss

The princess, following tradition, sought love among the amphibians of the local bog. She was careful about which she kissed. Only creatures exhibiting exceptional nobility, by their stature, or by the proud bearing they brought to their lily pad, could tempt her.

One afternoon, near despair at the absence of eligible toads, she spied an unremarkable animal some distance from the water. The King, she thought, is not so handsome, but he makes himself attractive by being always stand-offish. Perhaps this is what I should be seeking.

The aloof frog took no chasing, but hopped right to her. The princess scooped it up and took it to her lips. It croaked, shifted its weight forward and puckered up. She saw none of that, for it was her habit to close her eyes against the abject unpleasantness of the seldom magic peck. Their lips met. Instantly, she heard the frog's voice, as words this time, 'My darling, at last'.

She opened her eyes and gasped at the receiver of her kiss, still very much reptilian. 'B... b... but ... But in the story you transform into a handsome prince.'

'Strange,' replied the frog. 'We frogs have a similar tale. Though it seems, my pretty green one, that ours is the less fictitious.'

11.1

Activity

1 Explain the meaning of the following descriptions from the story in your own words.

a 'exhibiting exceptional nobility': ______________________

b 'absence of eligible toads': ______________________

c 'abject unpleasantness': ______________________

2 What is the 'tradition' referred to in the opening line of 'A Royal Kiss'?

____

____

3 How does 'A Royal Kiss' subvert (challenge) the features of traditional fairytales?

____

____

4 What is your impression of the princess based on her speech, dialogue and actions in this story? Describe the sort of person she is characterised as by the writer, providing evidence from the text.

____

____

____

____

5 According to the frog's final line of dialogue, what inference can you make about what happens to the princess after she kisses the frog?

____

____

Comprehension focus 2: summarising and inferring

The cartoon below was created by Ron Tandberg.

© Ron Tandbreg

11.2

Activity

1 In one sentence, summarise the main message of the cartoon.

____

____

2 Whose opinions and ideas do you think the cartoon is mocking? Explain why.

____

____

3 Complete the table below by describing the visual elements in the cartoon and summarising the effects (what does it make you think about or feel?) that each element may have on the reader.

Visual elements	Descriptions	Effects
sun	large, powerful-looking, dominates the picture	
men		Makes me think the men are blind to the possibility of solar energy; suggests businesses and mining companies are ignorant.
setting	desert-like environment, bare, no vegetation	
dialogue		

Comprehension focus 3: skimming, scanning and connecting

The following extract is from Simon Tong's short story 'The Beat of a Different Drum'.

I loved the pictures of dinosaurs and animals in the science books my uncle sent me from Taiwan, but I liked the pleasure of words even more. The rhythm of a mellifluous poem was honey on my tongue, the shape of a well-balanced *duilian* made me grin and grin. I won the school's essay competition every year; teachers marvelled at my vocabulary, rich and sophisticated for my age. I fantasised about growing up to become a writer.

…

My mother decided it was prudent for us to join the new wave of diaspora and we fled to Australia …

The sum total of what I knew about Australia came to three things: it had an opera house, kangaroos and Australians spoke the dreaded English …

My first day at school in Australia was stinking hot, the only kind of weather this desiccated country seemed to have … I was on a different planet. Even the thick air, superheated, utterly bereft of moisture (but so clean!), felt alien on my skin …

Robbed of speech again, but this time both inside and outside the classroom, I was stripped of my dignity and personality as well. I didn't have the words to object, to defend myself, to argue, to cajole or control. My ethnicity made me conspicuous, but my reticence made me invisible …

I discovered that soap operas were excellent learning aids: their plots universal and repetitive, the histrionic acting transpicuous; I could concentrate on the colloquial dialogues …

My relationship with English became a lot friendlier once I started to learn not just its grammar and vocabulary, but also to listen to its music.

11.3 Activity

1 **Skim** the extract and circle what text type you think it is from the options below.

biography   persuasive speech   feature article

autobiographical reflection   novel

2 Simon Tong has an obvious passion for language. **Scan** the extract and circle some words or phrases in the that suggest this interest.

skim Reading quickly, selecting key words and details through a text to determine the general meaning or main messages or ideas

scan To read, moving eyes quickly down a page, seeking specific words and phrases. It is also used when a reader first finds information to determine whether it will answer their questions

3 What do you think a '*duilian*' might be? Make a guess, then look it up. Why is it written in italics?

Your guess: ______________________________

Dictionary definition: ______________________________

Why is it in italics? ______________________________

4 What three things does the author know about Australia before arriving?

__________ __________ __________

5 How do you think Tong developed these expectations of Australia?

____

____

6 Re-read the paragraph that recounts Tong's first day at school and the paragraph following that. What factors contribute to his sense of alienation?

____

____

7 Why does Tong find watching soap operas helpful in learning 'colloquial dialogues'?

____

____

8 What was it that stripped Tong of his dignity and personality?

____

____

9 Have you ever been in a place or situation where you did not speak the dominant language? How did it make you feel?

____

____

10 The table below lists words used by Tong in the extract. Write the meaning of each word in the space provided.

Words from extract	Meanings
bereft	
cajole	
desiccated	
diaspora	
histrionic	
mellifluous	
prudent	
reticence	
transpicuous	

Comprehension focus 4: summarising, connecting and visualising

The following image is a reproduction of a famous painting created in 1955 by Australian artist John Brack. It depicts the afternoon peak hour in a Melbourne city street in the mid-1950s. The title of the painting is *Collins St, 5 p.m.*

11.4

Activity

1 Summarise your observations of the people in the foreground of *Collins St, 5 p.m.* Look closely at their faces and describe their collective features. Consider their facial expressions, gender, clothing and direction of travel.

2 Summarise your observations of the people in the background of the image.

3 List three **adjectives** to describe Brack's impression of peak hour in the city.

4 The painting has been created in sepia tones (shades of brown). Why do you think that Brack may have chosen this palette, or range of colours, for his painting?

The cartoon below was created by John Spooner and was published in *The Age* newspaper on 9 April 2010. It is titled *With Apology to John Brack.*

5 You may notice that Spooner has imitated many of the elements in the Brack painting. What is this practice of connecting one text to another through quotation, adaptation, parody or allusion called? Circle your answer from the options below.

extratextuality intertextuality intratextuality

6 What comment is Spooner making about Australian society in his cartoon?

7 Why do you think Spooner chose Brack's well-known painting to show his opinion of Australian society 55 years later?

8 Using Brack's painting as inspiration, create your own image that makes a comment or observation about modern Australian society. Consider the effects of social media, phone technology, the COVID-19 pandemic or other contextual factors.

adjective A word class that describes, identifies or quantifies a noun or a pronoun, e.g. two (number or quantity), my (possessive), ancient (descriptive), shorter (comparative), wooden (classifying)

Comprehension focus 5: activating prior knowledge, questioning and summarising

The text you are about to read is an extract from a news article titled 'Experts' Mind-blowing Predictions for Future of Travel in 2070', written by Chantelle Francis and published in April 2023. Complete the first question in Activity 11.5 before you read the text.

11.5

Activity

1 The contextual information tells you that the text you are about to read is a news article. Think about other news articles you have read. Based on your knowledge of news articles, which of the options listed below are features you might expect the text to include? Circle your answers.

headline characters setting

expert opinions and quotes formal language

Expect Hotels like Never Before

Imagine a digital holographic personal concierge waiting to greet you in your hotel lobby to tend to your every need. In 50 years it could be a reality.

You could also be choosing your room's decor to suit your taste, change the lighting, the music, the scent and the softness of your bed.

'A digital virtual room assistant (think Super-Alexa) will greet you and help you with anything from ordering a new towel to suggesting a place to eat and making a reservation for you,' futurist Shivvy Jervis said.

The buffet breakfasts of the future involve a digital menu where you can type in what you want to have 3D printed.

3D printed hotel buffet food could revolutionise breakfast and do away with waste.

By 2070, you could find yourself staying in an underwater hotel and going on a 'sea-fari' in a mini submarine, or you may stay underground with subterranean hotels expected to be built into the fabric of the earth.

And if you are not sure what holiday to go on or what to get up to one day, artificial intelligence is expected to be able to match you with the right destination, activity and even travelling companion.

For those who like to visit historical sites augmented reality will change the game. 'Forms of MR – mixed reality – will overlay images on the landscape to visually reconstruct what happened there: a famous battle, the troops surging around you, being sat among the cheering crowd at the very first Olympic Games,' Dr Sterry said.

It might be in the form of a projected hologram or by wearing a lightweight headset or glasses. Haptic suits could intensify the experience even further.

2 Highlight any words in the extract that you don't understand and record definitions or synonyms for them in the text margins.

3 Based on some of the predictions about what travel will be like in 2070, design three questions that you would like answered. An example has been provided for you.

Example question: Won't people's jobs be at risk if a 'holographic concierge' is waiting to greet visitors at a hotel instead of a real concierge?

Question 1: ____________________

____

Question 2: ____________________

____

Question 3: ____________________

____

Continue reading the news article below.

Look Back 50 Years

While the predictions might seem far-fetched now, lead expert Professor Birgitte Andersen said you only have to look back 50 years to realise it's all possible.

'Humanity has grown so accustomed to frequent beneficial advances in tech and engineering, that it can become easy to take for granted how far we've come in the last 50 years,' she wrote in the report's summary.

'Think back to 1973 – smartphones were a thing of wildest dreams, "Google" would have seemed like a made-up word, and laptops were still almost a decade away from being invented.

'It's unfathomable to us now to have lived in a world without these core technologies that are so fundamental to our being. So, when looking forward to the next 50 years, the potential possibilities for growth and development in innovation and technology for travel are endless.'

4 Summarise the main idea in the news article in one sentence.

____

____

5 Compile a list of questions that could be used to guide research for a news article titled 'Experts' Mind-blowing Predictions for Future of Education in 2070'. An example has been provided for you.

Example question: Will schools of the future still operate between approximately 9am and 3 pm?

____

____

____

____

____

____

Comprehension focus 6: skimming, scanning and connecting

The following extract comes from the opening chapter of *Mazin Grace*, the story of a young girl growing up on an Aboriginal mission in South Australia in the 1950s. The novel was written by Dylan Coleman.

My name is Grace. Grace Dawn. That's 'cause I was born just as the jindu came up over our Kokatha country on Koonibba Mission. Papa Neddy gave me my name. Said if it's good enough for Superintendent to call 'is girls Charity and Hope, it was good enough for me to 'ave a Bible name too. Mumma Jenna said she brought me into the world a year before that big war finished, just over a year after my sister Eva was born.

Ada, my mother, was my sister 'til I was about five years old. For Eva it was a bit older, before we knew the truth. Still call 'er Ada now, outa habit I s'pose. Can't say when I first knew that Papa Neddy and Mumma Jenna weren't really my parents but my grandparents, and that my big sisters were really my mothers, or 'aunties', as whitefellas call 'em. It was more a slow thing, like a ringworm. A minya faint circle on your skin, then itchin'. Could be mozzie bite, but before you know it, it's full grown and there's no mistaken'. It was kinda like that.

We got a big family, though, lotsa mothers and fathers, sisters and brothers. We all live in a little cottage on the Mission. There's lots cottages just like ours that other Nyunga families live in too. But not the Mission workers – Superintendent, Pastor, Nurse, Teacher. All them mob, they live in flash houses or nice rooms, not like ours. They different from us. They look at things different-wat, funny-way. I reckon they see things mixed-up way, sometimes. They don't understand our ways.

... We got another name too, it's Oldman. That's our last name. Papa says it came from way over the wanna in a big ship, from Ireland. Two twin brothers, one named Nat gave us 'is name through Granny Dianna, my Kokatha great grandmother, long time ago, when the walbiya mooga started comin' to our country.

Granny Dianna had a big strong brother, and he was a very special man Nyunga-way, 'is name mean the same as light from the moon. He taught Papa lotsa things. Papa always told us we 'ave a strong Kokatha bloodline that we must never forget and even though Mumma Jenna is Mirning and that blood runs through us too, we must hold strong to our Kokatha side, Papa's Mumma, Granny Dianna's side and 'er brother, that special one. That's how I've always known, proud-way- that I'm Kokatha.

That's what Papa taught us, that's what Granny Dianna and 'er brother Jumoo taught 'im. They always tell us this munda here and all the way 'wounds this way, where them rockholes are out that way, then back this way over to them other rockholes, and over that way to the Gawler Ranges, too. Big lot of Kokatha country and we gotta look after it, make sure it stays strong. Granny Dianna even got one rockhole same name as her, 'cause that's our country and she boss woman for all that place.

11.6 Activity

1 Although *Mazin Grace* is written largely in English, Coleman also uses words from the First Nations Kokatha language. Highlight the words in the extract that you think might be from the Kokatha language.

2 By considering the way in which the words are used in the passage, draw lines to match the Kokatha words on the left with their definitions on the right.

Kokatha words	Definitions
minya	ground
jindu	non-Aboriginal people
walbiya mooga	sun
wanna	Aboriginal person
munda	people from near the Great Australian Bight
Nyunga	small
Mirning	ocean

3 What is Grace's full name and why was she given that name?

4 When was Grace born and what significant event occurred at that time?

5 Who gave Grace her name and why did he choose a Bible name?

6 Who are Ada and Eva to Grace?

7 When did Grace find out the truth about her family?

8 What is the Mission and who lives there?

9 Why is it important for Grace and her family to hold strongly to their heritage?

10 What aspects of your heritage are important to you?

Comprehension focus 7: activating prior knowledge, connecting and visualising

The image below is a promotional poster for the film *Bridge to Terabithia,* based on a 1977 novel of the same name by Katherine Paterson.

11.7

Activity

1 What fantasy films or books have you viewed or read before?

____

____

2 The novel version of *Bridge to Terabithia* explores a fantasy world that the young characters in the story create for themselves. What visual elements of this fantasy world are apparent in this promotional poster for the film adaptation of the novel?

____

____

3 Draw or describe your own imaginary world in the space below, including the characters or creatures that live there.

Comprehension focus 8: inferring and connecting

The following text is an edited transcript of a 2009 TED Talk delivered by William Kamkwamba (his second TED Talk). His journey is also detailed in the book and film *The Boy Who Harnessed the Wind.* The speech can be viewed and listened to at https://www.ted.com/talks/william_kamkwamba_how_i_harnessed_the_wind

Two years ago, I stood on the TED stage in Arusha, Tanzania. I spoke very briefly about one of my proudest creations. It was a simple machine that changed my life.

Before that time, I had never been away from my home in Malawi. I had never used a computer. On the stage that day, I was so nervous. My English lost. I wanted to vomit. I had never been surrounded by so many azungu, white people.

There was a story I wouldn't tell you then. But well, I'm feeling good right now. I would like to share that story today. We have seven children in my family. All sisters, excepting me. Before I discovered the wonders of science, I was just a simple farmer in a country of poor farmers. Like everyone else, we grew maize.

One year our fortune turned very bad. In 2001 we experienced an awful famine. Within five months all Malawians began to starve to death. My family ate one meal per day, at night. Only three swallows of *nsima* for each one of us. The food passes through our bodies. We drop down to nothing.

In Malawi, the secondary school, you have to pay school fees. Because of the hunger, I was forced to drop out of school. I looked at my father and looked at those dry fields. It was the future I couldn't accept.

I was determined to do anything possible to receive education. So I went to a library. I read books, science books, especially physics. I couldn't read English that well. I used diagrams and pictures to learn the words around them.

Another book that put knowledge in my hands, it said a windmill could pump water and generate electricity.

Pump water meant irrigation, a defence against hunger, which we were experiencing at that time. So I decided I would build one windmill for myself. But I didn't have materials to use, so I went to a scrap yard where I found my materials. Many people, including my mother, said I was crazy.

I found a tractor fan, shock absorber, PVC pipes. Using a bicycle frame and an old bicycle dynamo, I built my machine. It was one light at first. And then four lights, with switches, and even a circuit breaker, modelled after an electric bell. Another machine pumps water for irrigation.

Queues of people start lining up at my house to charge their mobile phone. I could not get rid of them. And the reporters came too, which led to bloggers and which led to a call from something called TED. I had never seen a plane before. I have never slept in a hotel. So, on stage that day in Arusha, my English lost, I said something like, 'I tried. And I made it.'

So I would like to say something to all the people out there like me, to the Africans and the poor who are struggling with your dreams. God bless. Maybe one day you will watch this on the Internet. I say to you, trust yourself and believe. Whatever happened, don't give up. Thank you.

11.8

Activity

1 How did William's experience of famine impact his education and future aspirations?

____

____

2 How did William teach himself about windmills and their potential uses?

____

____

3 In what ways did William's creation of a windmill change his life and the lives of those around him?

____

____

4 How does the speech connect to themes of perseverance and resilience?

____

____

5 How might the story that William shares inspire others who face similar challenges to pursue their dreams and believe in themselves?

____

____

6 How does William's experience compare with the experiences of other individuals who have faced challenges trying to get an education? Provide examples to support your answer.

____

____

7 Watch a range of other TED Talks based on the topic of education or overcoming challenges and complete the following comparison chart. Compare each TED Talk with William Kamkwamba's speech.

8 Which of the speakers you listened to demonstrated the most effective control of features of voice, such as pitch, volume, pace and inflection? Provide reasons for your answer.

TED Talk titles	Similar ideas and opinions	Differences in ideas and opinions
TED Talk 1:		
TED Talk 2:		
TED Talk 3:		

Improving your writing

This unit targets the knowledge and skills that will help improve the quality of your writing. Each activity is designed to help you revise or learn about a particular language feature or grammar convention. Understanding the different parts of speech – such as nouns and adjectives – and the way sentences are structured will enable you to communicate clearly with readers. There are lots of opportunities for you to apply your understanding of literacy and language in the writing activities in this unit.

language features Features that support meaning (e.g. clause- and word-level grammar, vocabulary, figurative language, punctuation, images). Choices vary for the purpose, subject matter, audience and mode or medium

convention An accepted practice that has developed over time and is generally used and understood (e.g. use of punctuation)

Curriculum content

Australian Curriculum content description	Content code
Investigate a range of cohesive devices that condense information in texts, including nominalisation, and devices that link, expand and develop ideas, including text connectives.	AC9E9LA04
Understand how abstract nouns and nominalisation can be used to summarise ideas in text.	AC9E9LA06
Understand how spelling is used in texts for particular effects; for example, characterisation, humour and to represent accents and distinctive speech.	AC9E8LY08

Punctuation

Punctuation marks are sometimes called 'the traffic signals of language'. They tell us when to slow down, when to pay particular attention to something, when to take a detour or when to stop. Punctuation is very important for making meaning clear in both written and spoken language.

Commas

A comma indicates a short pause in a sentence. Commas are used to separate items in a list or to separate a series of thoughts or actions. They also separate a main clause from a subordinate clause in a sentence when the subordinate clause comes first. (Clauses are covered later in this unit.) A comma may also be used after an introductory word or phrase, such as 'However', 'Therefore' or 'On the other hand'.

12.1

Activity

1 Add commas in the correct places in the sentences below.

a I love Geography History and Indonesian.

b At recess I followed my friends to the canteen.

c *Batman* is my favourite film. However *Star Wars* comes a close second.

d Angie Rae Surinda and Mae are all coming to my party on the weekend.

2 Write your own sentence that demonstrates an understanding of how commas can be used in a list.

____

____

3 Write your own sentence that demonstrates an understanding of how a comma can be used to separate a main and subordinate clause.

____

____

4 Write your own sentence that demonstrates an understanding of how a comma can be used after an introductory word or phrase.

____

____

Colons

Colons are used at the end of clauses to amplify or introduce the information that follows. They are also sometimes used to introduce direct speech or a list. One way of remembering when to use a colon is by asking yourself the question, 'Could the words "that is" be used instead?' If the answer is 'Yes', then a colon is appropriate. The answer to this question is 'Yes' in the following examples.

» There was only one thing to do: run.

» The principal called out a final piece of advice: 'Never forget where you came from.'

» I have a lot of hobbies: playing guitar, cooking and reading.

A colon gives emphasis to whatever you're introducing because readers must come to a stop, which leads them to give greater attention to the details that follow.

colon Punctuation mark (:) that separates a general statement from one or more statements that give extra information, explanation or illustration. Statements after a colon do not have to be full sentences

12.2 Activity

1 Add colons in the correct places in the sentences below.

a I'd lived in the street only a week, but I already knew the names of my next-door neighbour's cats Minky, Lulu, Fluffy and Whiskas.

b I was so nervous on my first day working at the bakery that I couldn't even answer my manager's first question 'Have you used a cash register before?'

c As soon as I've saved enough money, I am going to travel to some of Australia's most famous landmarks Uluru, the Sydney Opera House and the Twelve Apostles.

2 Write your own sentence that demonstrates an understanding of how a colon can be used to introduce a list.

____

____

3 Write your own sentence that demonstrates an understanding of how a colon can be used to amplify or emphasise the information that follows.

____

____

Semicolons

Semicolons have two uses:

» They separate two main clauses that are closely connected in meaning when a **conjunction** (like 'and' or 'but') is not used. For example: 'I had always liked meat; my brother was the vegetarian in the house.'

- They separate items in a list when the items already have commas included in them. For example: 'My favourite foods are spicy chilli, chicken and coconut soup; lemon, ginger and garlic stir-fry; and pasta with dill, capers and salmon.'

One effective way of deciding whether to use a semicolon in sentences like the first example above is to imagine the words in each part of the sentence being placed on a scale. If the two sides balance, or make sense without the other half, then both parts of the sentences are main clauses and can be separated by a semicolon.

semicolon Punctuation (;) used to join closely related clauses that could stand alone as sentences and can be used to separate long items in a list
conjunction In a sentence, a word that joins other words, groups/phrases or clauses together in a logical relationship such as addition, time, cause or comparison. There are 2 types: coordinating and subordinating

12.3

Activity

1. Add semicolons in the correct places in the sentences below.
   a. I have to tell my mother it will make her really proud.
   b. Stewart was in my Science class we both supported Real Madrid.
   c. I always wanted to be able to play the flute like Sian she thought it was cool that I could speak three languages.
   d. She loves to read books he prefers to watch movies.
   e. Contributors to the book *Growing Up Asian in Australia* include Shaun Tan, who won the Astrid Lindgren Memorial Award in 2011 for his work as an illustrator of children's books Annette Shun Wah, prominent media personality Jenny Kee, one-time model and fashion designer and John So, the second-longest-serving Lord Mayor of Melbourne.
2. Write your own sentence that uses a semicolon to separate two main clauses.

____

____

3. Write your own sentence that uses semicolons to separate list items that have commas in them.

____

____

Ellipses

An ellipsis (…) is used to show that material has been left out of a quotation. It can also be used in **narrative** texts to create suspense or to indicate hesitation, surprise or an incomplete thought. The plural form of ellipsis is 'ellipses'.

narrative The selection and sequencing of events or experiences, real or imagined, to tell a story to entertain, engage, inform and extend imagination, typically using an orientation, complication and resolution

12.4 Activity

1 Explain the impression created by the ellipsis in each of the following sentences.

a 'Did you just delete the whole folder?'

'Ah. I did … I think.'

b I looked around the auditorium at the sea of hands in the air. Please, please choose me …

c I can't believe it … he actually passed the test!

2 Write your own sentence that uses an ellipsis to indicate hesitation.

3 Write your own sentence that uses an ellipsis to create suspense.

Expanding your vocabulary

It is important to work on expanding your vocabulary so that you can communicate more effectively in both your writing and your speaking. A wide vocabulary will help you to express yourself more easily and precisely. It will also assist you to understand the meaning of what others are saying or what you are reading. There are many strategies that you can use to expand your vocabulary, including:

- reading widely: try to challenge yourself with a range of books, magazines, online content and newspapers
- learning a new word every day: there are lots of apps that will send you an uncommon word and its definition daily
- doing crosswords, playing Scrabble or other vocabulary games
- using a thesaurus to find suitable **synonyms**
- keeping a glossary of unfamiliar words and their definitions as you encounter them through reading or conversation.

synonym A word having nearly the same meaning as others (e.g. synonyms for 'old' include 'aged', 'venerable', 'antiquated')

12.5 Activity

1 Draw lines to match the following challenging words with their definitions.

euphoria	a problem that is difficult to solve
conundrum	a feeling of intense happiness or excitement
soporific	a statement that contradicts itself
prodigy	able to deal with something in a sensible, practical way
paradox	mentally sharp, clever or observant
astute	inducing sleep or drowsiness
pragmatic	a young person with an exceptional talent or ability

2 Using a thesaurus, find synonyms for the following words.

a good: ____________________

b bad: ____________________

c nice: ____________________

d big: ____________________

e small: ____________________

f happy: ____________________

g sad: ____________________

3 Find a piece of writing that you did recently. In the left-hand column of the table below, list some words from your work that you overused or that were imprecise. Then, in the right-hand columns, write some interesting synonyms for each word. You can use a thesaurus. Some examples have been provided for you.

Words	Synonyms		
walk	amble	meander	promenade

4 Create a short, descriptive piece of writing that includes some of the alternative words you have added to the table above.

____

____

____

____

____

12.6

Activity

The following word pairs are often confused, even by computer spell-checkers, which often select the wrong one! Using a proper dictionary, find the meanings of the words below and construct separate sentences that demonstrate an understanding of their different meanings.

1 conscious/conscience

a Meaning of conscious: _______________

b Meaning of conscience: _______________

c Sentence 1 (conscious): _______________

____

d Sentence 2 (conscience): _______________

____

2 scarred/scared

a Meaning of scarred: _______________

b Meaning of scared: _______________

c Sentence 1 (scarred): _______________

____

d Sentence 2 (scared): ______________________________

____

3 vicious/viscous

a Meaning of vicious: ______________________________

b Meaning of viscous: ______________________________

c Sentence 1 (vicious): ______________________________

____

d Sentence 2 (viscous): ______________________________

____

4 loose/lose

a Meaning of loose: ______________________________

b Meaning of lose: ______________________________

c Sentence 1 (loose): ______________________________

____

d Sentence 2 (lose): ______________________________

____

5 principle/principal

a Meaning of principle: ______________________________

b Meaning of principal: ______________________________

c Sentence 1 (principle): ______________________________

____

d Sentence 2 (principal): ______________________________

____

6 access/assess

a Meaning of access: ______________________________

b Meaning of assess: ______________________________

c Sentence 1 (access): ______________________________

____

d Sentence 2 (assess): ______________________________

____

Unconventional spelling

At times, authors use unconventional or deliberately incorrect spelling in order to produce certain effects. For instance, they might spell words in an unusual way to represent a character's accent or distinctive way of speaking, to generate humour or to respond to changes in society when new words are made.

Creating character

By using unconventional spelling to represent the unique voices and accents of characters, authors can make their stories more engaging and their characters more authentic. The spelling may be phonetic, meaning that it is based on the sounds made, rather than following conventional spelling rules. For example:

» 'Ya'll come back now, ya hear?' (Southern American accent)

» 'Whaddya mean, youse guys?' (New York City accent)

» 'G'day mate, how ya goin'?' (Australian accent)

12.7

Activity

1 Create some lines of dialogue that indicate by deliberate misspellings the different accents of two characters.

____

____

____

Sometimes, unconventional spelling can reveal other information about a character, such as their age, social class or level of education. Authors may deliberately drop letters from words or alter their spelling to mimic the sound of characters' natural spoken words.

2 Circle the spelling 'errors' in the lines of dialogue below. For each line of dialogue, explain what you can infer about the speaker based on the deliberate misspelling of dialogue or writing that an author has assigned to them. Consider their likely age, social class or level of education.

'I ain't got no money.' ______________________________

'Skool waddn't eva my jam.' _________________________

'Nah, I don't feel like eating, bro.' ______________________

Neologisms

A neologism is a new word or expression that becomes commonly used. Neologisms often appear as a result of emerging trends, new technology or significant cultural events. For instance, the term 'iso' became popularly used and accepted during the COVID-19 pandemic as a way of referring to isolation and mandatory quarantine, and the word 'selfie' emerged as a result of smartphone technology allowing people to take photos of themselves easily.

12.8 Activity

1 Search the internet, social media or other sources and record a list of neologisms in the table below. Include definitions for each. An example has been provided for you.

Neologisms	Definitions
nepo baby	the children of celebrities who are perceived to be unfairly advantaged by 'piggybacking' off the success of their parents

Neologisms can be created by combining existing words or by altering the pronunciation or spelling of words.

2 What words have been combined to create the following neologisms? You may need to research some of these to answer correctly.

a brunch: ______

b paralympics: ______

c infotainment: ______

d chillax: ______

e cli-fi: ______

Concrete and abstract nouns

Concrete nouns refer to tangible things that can be physically seen, touched, tasted, heard or smelled. Some examples are tree, cup, dog, apple and music. By contrast, abstract nouns refer to intangible concepts, ideas or qualities that cannot be experienced through the senses. They include love, happiness, justice and freedom. While we can't physically see, touch, taste, hear or smell these things, we can see evidence of them in action and observe their effects on us.

12.9

Activity

1 Decide whether the following words are concrete or abstract nouns and white them in the correct columns in the table below.

love	book	justice	table	trust
water	freedom	phone	beauty	chair
wisdom	car	fear	music	computer
friendship	hatred	rock	honesty	television
curiosity				

Concrete nouns	Abstract nouns

2 Brainstorm five extra concrete nouns and five extra abstract nouns. Add them to the table above.

Abstract nouns can be used to summarise ideas succinctly. In fact, you probably already practise summarising the main **themes** or ideas in the texts you read or view in class using abstract nouns. For example, you might identify that the main theme in something you read or watch is friendship, love or loyalty.

theme The main idea, concept or message of a text

3 Highlight the abstract nouns in the sentences below.

a *The Great Gatsby* by F. Scott Fitzgerald explores the concept of disillusionment with the American Dream, as characters grapple to achieve love, wealth and social status.

b *To Kill a Mockingbird* by Harper Lee examines the concepts of justice, prejudice and courage, as a lawyer defends a black man in a racially charged trial.

4 In one sentence, summarise the themes in a text you have recently read or viewed, using abstract nouns in your sentence.

____

____

Nominalisation

Nominalisation is a language technique in which a **verb** or **adjective** is turned into a noun. For example, the verb 'explore' can be turned into the noun 'exploration', and the adjective 'important' can be turned into the noun 'importance'. Nominalisation can help to make writing clearer and more concise by summarising complex ideas.

verb A word class that expresses processes that include doing, feeling, thinking, saying and relating
adjective A word class that describes, identifies or quantifies a noun or a pronoun, e.g. two (number or quantity), my (possessive), ancient (descriptive), shorter (comparative), wooden (classifying)

12.10

Activity

1 Rewrite the following sentences to include nominalisation. The verbs or adjectives that could be nominalised are underlined. The first one has been done for you.

a The <u>beautiful</u> painting captured everyone's attention.

Nominalisation: The painting's beauty captured everyone's attention.

b The teacher <u>explained</u> to the class how to solve the problem.

____

____

c The scientists <u>experimented</u> for weeks trying to find the cure.

____

____

d My brother finally <u>admitted</u> that he had taken the last lolly.

____

____

2 Brainstorm a list of adjectives and verbs that could be nominalised. An example of each has been provided for you.

Adjectives that can be nominalised	Verbs that can be nominalised
fashionable	transforming

3 Write a short paragraph that includes five different words from the table in the previous question in their nominalised form.

____

____

____

____

Cohesive devices

Cohesive devices include nominalisation and other devices that link, expand and develop ideas, including text connectives. **Cohesion** is important in all texts, but in persuasive, analytical and argumentative texts in particular, the reader or listener needs to be able to follow a logical line of argument.

> **cohesion** Grammatical or lexical relationships that bind different parts of a text together and give it unity. It is achieved through devices such as reference, substitution, repetition and text connectives

Connectives

Connectives are words or **phrases** that connect one idea to the next. They can also be a way of introducing additional examples to support your point. To develop an idea further using connectives, you can use some of the following sentence starters.

- In addition, …
- Furthermore, …
- Moreover, …
- Additionally, …
- Also, …

> **connective** Words linking and logically relating ideas to one another in paragraphs and sentences, indicating relationships of time, cause and effect, comparison, addition, condition and concession or clarification
>
> **phrase** A group of words often beginning with a preposition but without a subject and verb combination (e.g. 'on the river'; 'with brown eyes')

12.11

Activity

1 Write the introduction to a persuasive essay that makes an argument either for or against one of the topics listed below. The introduction should outline three main points to support your argument. Make sure you use connectives to introduce each additional point.

a Social media should have stricter rules.

b Artificial intelligence is more harmful than helpful.

c The school day should start later.

2 Highlight the connectives you used to create cohesion in your introduction above.

Refutations

Sometimes a persuasive response, for example, in a debate or an opinion piece, will consider the other side of an argument in order to refute it. Refutation involves giving attention to an opposing viewpoint in order to reject it or highlight how it is flawed. When you need to refute an argument and introduce the other side, these sentence starters are useful.

- Some people believe, however, …
- Despite these objections, …
- On the other hand, there are those who argue that …
- Others will argue that …
- Despite the facts, there are those who claim …
- Nevertheless, it is clear that …

12.12 Activity

Write a short paragraph that offers a counterargument (or refutation) to the argument you introduced for the previous activity. Make sure you begin with one of the sentence starters above.

Conditionals

Conditionals are words or phrases used to indicate that something will happen only if a certain condition is met. They can be used to connect ideas in a cause-and-effect relationship, showing how one idea leads to another based on the condition. They can also be used to present alternative outcomes based on different conditions. Some examples of conditionals are:

if	when	unless	as long as
in case	provided that	even if	whether or not

12.13

Activity

1 Complete the following sentences by adding an appropriate conditional word or phrase from the list above in the space provided. There may be more than one correct answer.

a ____________________ we don't take action to reduce greenhouse gas emissions, the consequences for the planet will be catastrophic.

b ____________________ we invest more in renewable energy, we'll continue to be dependent on fossil fuels.

c ____________________ you don't believe in climate change, it's still important to take steps to protect the environment for future generations.

d ____________________ we invest in our schools, we can ensure a brighter future for our children.

e ____________________ you support tougher penalties on crime, we can all agree the issue needs attention.

2 Create three of your own sentences that include some of the conditional words or phrases listed above, based on the topic you selected to write about in your introduction and refutation in the previous activities.

____

____

____

____

____

____

Indicating conclusions

Another way of achieving cohesion in your persuasive writing or speaking is to indicate that you have reached a conclusion on a given topic. The following sentence starters provide an effective way for you to confidently show that you have proved your points and arrived at a clear conclusion.

- There can surely be no doubt that …
- It must, therefore, be clear that …
- No responsible person could disagree that …
- Clearly, then, it is the case that …
- Undoubtedly, then, it is apparent that …

12.14

Activity

Write a concluding sentence for the topic that you selected to write about in your introduction, refutation and conditional sentences in the previous activities. Make sure you begin with one of the sentence starters listed above.

____

____

____

Sentence structures

Sentences that are varied in length and structure can convey ideas and feelings effectively. In written form, a sentence should always start with a capital letter and contain a clear meaning on its own. There are four main types of sentences:

- a statement (e.g. It's going to be another wet and gloomy day.)
- a question (e.g. Do you think I'll need an umbrella later?)
- an instruction (e.g. Bring me the umbrella from the boot of the car.)
- an exclamation (e.g. This constant rain is so annoying!)

12.15

Activity

Write your own example of each of the following types of sentences.

1 statement:

____

____

2 question:

____

____

3 instruction:

____

____

4 exclamation:

____

____

Clauses

A **clause** is a group of words containing a **subject** and a verb. An independent (or main) clause is a group of words containing a subject and a verb that can stand alone as a simple sentence.

In the simple sentences below, the subjects are underlined and the verbs are in italics.

» <u>Our team</u> *won*.

» <u>The other team</u> *lost*.

A dependent clause (or subordinate clause) is a group of words containing a subject and a verb that cannot stand alone because it does not contain a complete idea. Here are some examples, in which the dependent clause is italicised.

» Our team won *by keeping our eyes on the ball*.

» *When the siren sounded*, we were ten goals ahead.

» Our morale, *now that we were no longer on the bottom of the ladder*, improved significantly.

clause A grammatical unit referring to a happening or state e.g. 'the team won' (happening), 'the dog is red' (state), usually containing a subject and a verb group/phrase
subject A word or group of words (usually a noun group/phrase) in a sentence or clause representing the person, thing or idea doing the action that follows (e.g. 'The dog [subject] was barking')

12.16

Activity

1 Underline the independent clauses and circle the dependent clauses in the sentences below.

a Although I love to eat fast food, I know it's not good for my health.

b Because it was raining so heavily, we decided to stay indoors and watch a movie.

c The movie, which I had been waiting months to see, turned out to be a huge disappointment.

d Since he had a meeting early in the morning, he went to bed early last night.

e I always make sure that I wear sunscreen to protect my skin whenever I go to the beach.

2 Using the examples above as models, create your own sentences that include a dependent clause in the positions identified below.

a at the beginning of the sentence:

____

____

b in the middle of the sentence:

____

____

c at the end of the sentence:

____

____

Compound and complex sentences

A **compound sentence** consists of two or more independent clauses joined together by a semi colon or a conjunction (joining word). A **complex sentence** contains one independent clauses and one or more dependent clauses that provide more information.

compound sentence A sentence with 2 or more main clauses of equal grammatical status, usually marked by a coordinating conjunction, e.g. [Ira came home this morning] [but he didn't stay long]
complex sentence A sentence with one or more subordinate clauses. In the following example, the subordinate clause is shown in brackets: I took my umbrella [because it was raining]

12.17

Activity

1 The following examples are opening sentences from novels. Each one is an example of either a complex sentence or a compound sentence. Identify whether each sentence is complex or compound and circle the correct answer.

a The dog we're betting on looks more like a rat. (complex or compound?)

b One damp, silvery afternoon, an old lady came home from walking her dog and found a boy sitting on the floral settee. (complex or compound?)

c We were, I guess, about one-third of the way up the silo when my knees and elbows locked. (complex or compound?)

d Whether I shall turn out to be the hero of my own life, or whether that station will be held by anybody else, these pages must show. (complex or compound?)

e If you really want to hear about it, the first thing you'll probably want to know is where I was born, and what my lousy childhood was like, how my parents were occupied and all before they had me, and all that David Copperfield kind of crap, but I don't feel like going into it, if you want to know the truth. (complex or compound?)

2 Write your own examples of a compound and a complex sentence below.

a a compound sentence:

____

____

b a complex sentence:

____

____

Sentence fragments

A sentence fragment is a group of words that lacks a complete idea. It is not considered a full sentence. It might lack a noun or verb, or it might be a dependent clause separated from an independent clause. The fragment might even be a single, isolated word. Fragments are generally not used in formal or academic **styles** of writing. However, fiction writers, as well as speech-makers, take liberties with sentences and fragments to create certain effects.

style The distinctive language features, text structures and/or subject matter in a text which may shape meaning, be enjoyed for its aesthetic qualities or distinguish the work of an author, period etc.

12.18 Activity

1 Read the following two passages. For each one, write your observations about how the sentence fragments are used to craft a powerful description.

a First impressions? Misleading, of course. As always. But unforgettable: the red glow of his face – a boozer's incandescent glow. The pitted, sun-coarsened skin – a cheap, ruined leather. And the eyes: an old man's moist, wobbling jellies. (*Maestro*, Peter Goldsworthy)

____

____

b Our home's gone. Bulldozed. Bloke that owned it, sold it. Bloke that bought it, knocked it down. Another bloke cemented it up. Poured a big slab of concrete over our front yard, then over our back yard, then poured cement on everything in between ... Concreted over all the teasings and fights and tears, over the headaches and heartaches and long, lazy nights. (*Njunjul the Sun*, Meme McDonald and Boori Monty Pryor)

Varying sentence structures and lengths

Varying the structures and lengths of sentences can have the effect of making your writing more engaging. Short sentences and sentence fragments can work to build suspense or place emphasis on their words. Lengthy sentences can be used to slow the pace of reading. A combination of simple, compound and complex sentences can maintain reader interest and prevent a monotonous effect.

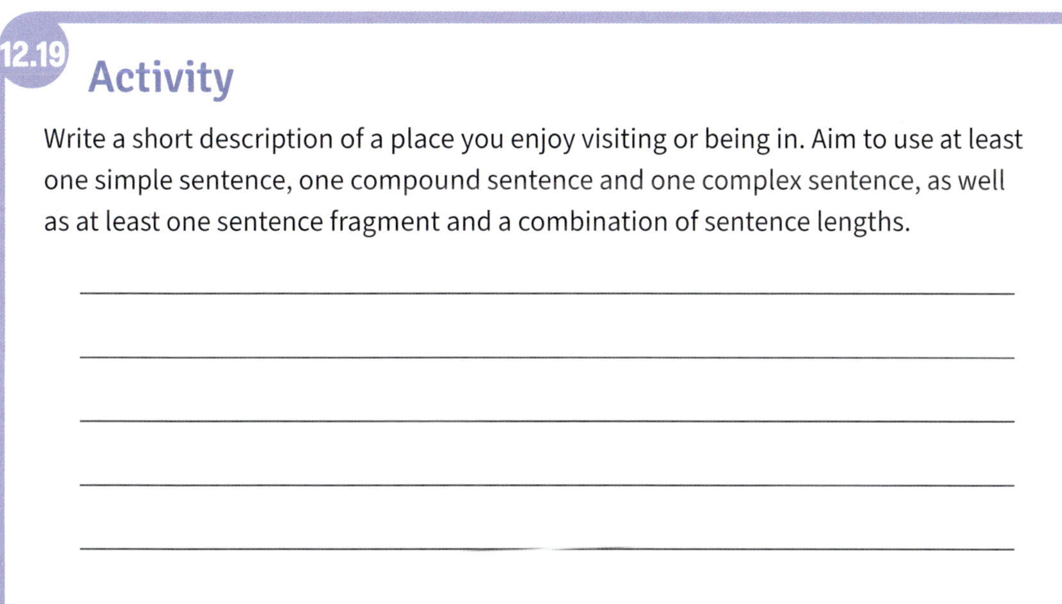

12.19

Activity

Write a short description of a place you enjoy visiting or being in. Aim to use at least one simple sentence, one compound sentence and one complex sentence, as well as at least one sentence fragment and a combination of sentence lengths.

Glossary

adjective A word class that describes, identifies or quantifies a noun or a pronoun, e.g. two (number or quantity), my (possessive), ancient (descriptive), shorter (comparative), wooden (classifying).

adverb A word class that may modify a verb (e.g. 'softly' in 'the boy sings softly'), an adjective (e.g. 'really' in 'he is really strong') or another adverb (e.g. 'very' in 'the toddler walks very slowly').

aesthetic Concerned with a sense of beauty or an appreciation of artistic expression.

alliteration A recurrence of the same consonant sounds at the beginning of words in close succession (e.g. 'ripe, red raspberry').

assonance The repetition of vowel sounds within words (e.g. rain, main).

attitudes Particular ways of thinking and feeling towards people or things.

audience An intended or assumed group of readers, listeners or viewers that a writer, designer, filmmaker or speaker is addressing.

cinematography The science and art of shooting motion-picture scenes, including the camera work and lighting.

clause A grammatical unit referring to a happening or state e.g. 'the team won' (happening), 'the dog is red' (state), usually containing a subject and a verb group/phrase.

cohesion Grammatical or lexical relationships that bind different parts of a text together and give it unity. It is achieved through devices such as reference, substitution, repetition and text connectives.

colon Punctuation mark (:) that separates a general statement from one or more statements that give extra information, explanation or illustration. Statements after a colon do not have to be full sentences.

complex sentence A sentence with one or more subordinate clauses. In the following example, the subordinate clause is shown in brackets: I took my umbrella [because it was raining].

compound sentence A sentence with 2 or more main clauses of equal grammatical status, usually marked by a coordinating conjunction, e.g. [Ira came home this morning] [but he didn't stay long].

comprehension strategies Processes used by readers to make meaning from texts. They include activating and using prior knowledge, predicting likely future events in a text, monitoring meaning and critically reflecting.

conjunction In a sentence, a word that joins other words, groups/phrases or clauses together in a logical relationship such as addition, time, cause or comparison. There are 2 types: coordinating and subordinating.

connective Words linking, and logically relating ideas to one another, in paragraphs and sentences indicating relationships of time, cause and effect, comparison, addition, condition and concession or clarification.

context An environment or situation (social, cultural or historical) in which a text is responded to or created. Or wording surrounding an unfamiliar word, which a reader or listener uses to understand its meaning.

contraction An abbreviated version of a word or words, often formed by shortening a word or merging 2 words into one (e.g. doctor: Dr; do not: don't).

convention An accepted practice that has developed over time and is generally used and understood (e.g. use of punctuation).

dialect Form of a language distinguished by features of vocabulary, grammar and pronunciation particular to a region.

edit To prepare, alter, adapt or refine with attention to grammar, spelling, punctuation and vocabulary.

hybrid text A composite text resulting from a purposeful mixing of elements from different sources or genres (e.g. 'infotainment').

idiom An expression whose meaning does not relate to the literal meaning of its words (e.g. 'They went out to paint the town red').

imagery Visually descriptive or figurative language to represent things including objects, actions and ideas in ways that appeal to the senses of the reader or viewer.

imperative verb A verb that gives an order or instruction (e.g. 'open the door').

jargon Technical words specific to a certain group, such as medical or legal jargon.

language features Features that support meaning e.g. clause- and word-level grammar, vocabulary, figurative language, punctuation, images. Choices vary for the purpose, subject matter, audience and mode or medium.

literary text Past and contemporary texts across a range of cultural contexts which are valued for their form and style and are recognised as having artistic value.

metalanguage Vocabulary including technical terms, concepts, ideas or codes used to describe or discuss a language. The language of grammar and the language of literary criticism are examples.

metaphor A type of figurative language used to describe a person or object through an implicit comparison to something with similar characteristics.

mise en scène In film, the composition of a shot, including elements such as lighting, costumes, props, set design and special effects.

modal verb A verb that expresses a degree of probability attached by a speaker or writer to a statement (e.g. 'I might come home') or a degree of obligation (e.g. 'You must give it to me').

mode Various processes of communication – listening, speaking, reading or viewing and writing or creating.

multimodal A combination of 2 or more communication modes (e.g. print, image and spoken text, as in film or computer presentations).

narrative The selection and sequencing of events or experiences, real or imagined, to tell a story to entertain, engage, inform and extend imagination, typically using an orientation, complication and resolution.

noun A word class that includes all words denoting person, place, object or thing, idea or emotion. Nouns may be common, proper, collective, abstract and compound.

perspective A lens through which the author perceives the world and creates a text, or the lens through which the reader or viewer perceives the world and understands a text.

phrase A group of words often beginning with a preposition but without a subject and verb combination (e.g. 'on the river'; 'with brown eyes').

point of view The position from which the text is designed to be perceived (e.g. a narrator might take a role of first or third person, omniscient or restricted in knowledge of events or the opinion presented in a text)

prefix A meaningful element (morphemes) added to the beginning of a word to change its meaning (e.g. 'un' to 'happy' to make 'unhappy').

preposition A word class that usually describes the relationship between words in a sentence. Prepositions can indicate space (e.g. 'on'), time (e.g. 'after') and other relationships (e.g. 'of', 'except').

prepositional phrase A group of words that typically consists of a preposition followed by a noun group/ phrase (e.g. 'on the train' in 'we met on the train'; 'on golf' in 'keen on golf').

pronoun A word that takes the place of a noun (e.g. I, me, he, she, herself, you, it, that, they, few, many, who, whoever, someone, everybody, and many others).

protagonist The main character in a text.

purpose An intended or assumed reason for a type of text.

salience A strategy of emphasis, highlighting what is important in a text. In images, it is achieved through strategies such as the placement of an item in the foreground, size and contrast in tone or colour.

scan To read, moving one's eyes quickly down a page seeking specific words and phrases. It is also used when a reader first finds information to determine whether it will answer their questions.

semicolon Punctuation (;) used to join closely related clauses that could stand alone as sentences and can be used to separate long items in a list.

simile A device comparing 2 things that are not alike. Similes use 'like', 'as' or 'than' to make the comparison (e.g. The cake was as light as air).

skim Reading quickly, selecting key words and details through a text to determine the general meaning or main messages or ideas.

Standard Australian English Recognised as the 'common language' of Australians, it is the dynamic and evolving spoken and written English used for official or public purposes, and recorded in dictionaries, style guides and grammars.

style The distinctive language features, text structures and/ or subject matter in a text which may shape meaning, be enjoyed for its aesthetic qualities or distinguish the work of an author, period etc.

subject A word or group of words (usually a noun group/ phrase) in a sentence or clause representing the person, thing or idea doing the action that follows (e.g. 'The dog [subject] was barking').

subject matter The topic or theme under consideration.

subordinating conjunction Words that introduce clauses that add or extend information. They include conjunctions such as 'after', 'when', 'because', 'if' and 'that'.

suffix An element added to the end of a word to change its meaning (e.g. to form past tense: '-ed'; to show a smaller amount or degree: -less; to form an adverb: -ly).

symbolism The use of one object, person or situation to signify or represent another by giving them meanings that are different from their literal sense (e.g. a dove is a symbol of peace).

synonym A word having nearly the same meaning as others (e.g. synonyms for 'old' include 'aged', 'venerable', 'antiquated').

tense The form a verb takes to signal the location of a clause in time (e.g. present tense 'has' in 'Jo has a cat' locates the situation in the present; past tense 'had' in 'Jo had a cat' locates it in the past).

theme The main idea, concept or message of a text.

tone The mood created by the language features used by an author and the way the text makes the reader feel.

values Ideas and beliefs specific to individuals and groups.

verb A word class that expresses processes that include doing, feeling, thinking, saying and relating.

verb group Consists of a main verb, alone or preceded by one or more auxiliary or modal verbs as modifiers.

visual features Visual components of a text which may include placement, salience, framing, representation of action or reaction, shot size, social distance and camera angle.

voice The distinct personality of a piece of writing; the individual writing style of the composer, created through the way they use and mix various language features (e.g. a narrative using a child's voice).

Acknowledgements

Insight Publications thanks the following writers for their contributions to *Australian Curriculum English Year 9*: Leanne Bondin and Adam Kealley.

Insight Publications is also grateful to the following individuals and organisations for permission to reproduce copyright material.

Texts: 'She's Gone' by Pat Flynn in *A Collection of Interesting Short Stories and Other Stuff from Some Surprising and Intelligent People*, Lili Wilkinson (editor), Fitzroy: Black Dog Books, 2008; 'February 12' © Erinn Pascal, 2015. Micro-story by Freya Cox, Year 9 in *Creating Micro-Stories* (2019), Boas and Jenkins, AATE November 2019; 'The Old Nurse's Story' by Elizabeth Gaskell, 1852; 'Redfern Speech' by Paul Keating, December 1992; 'The Surfer' by Judith Wright, 'The Road Not Taken' by Robert Frost; 'White Stucco Dreaming' by Samuel Wagan Watson; Extracts from *A Walk in the Dark* by Jane Godwin, Hachette Australia, 2022; Extracts from 'Hippotherapy' by Alistair Baldwin in *Growing Up Disabled in Australia* edited by Carly Findlay. Black Inc, 2021; 'The Drover's Wife' by Henry Lawson; 'Angus' by Loki Liddle, © Loki Liddle; Extracts from *YOLO JULIET* by Brett Wright and William Shakespeare, by Random House LLC. Used by permission of Random House Children's Books, a division of Penguin Random House LLC.; 'A Royal Kiss' © Richard Holt, 2016; 'Experts' mind blowing predictions for future of travel in 2070', by Chantelle Francis, news.com.au; Extract: 'The beat of a different drum' by Simon Tong, in *Growing up Asian in Australia*, Black Inc.; Extract from 'Mazin Grace' © Dylan Coleman, 2012, reprinted by permission; TED Talk by William Kamkwamba;

Images: Film poster, 'Monster House', Alamy; Film still, 'Edward Scissorhands'; Image, Tim Burton and Helena Bonham Carter, Alamy; Film poster, 'Gurrumul'; Film poster, 'Planet Earth'; Film poster, 'He named me Malala'; Film poster, 'Blue'; Film poster, 'In my blood it runs' ; Image, Alistair Baldwin; Citizenship ceremony, Cardinia Council; Play poster, 'An excellent conceited tragedie of Romeo and Iuliet', Alamy, Cartoon, 'There must be a source of energy down there' © Ron Tandberg; 'Collins St, 5 p.m.', by John Brack, National Gallery of Victoria, Melbourne, purchased in 1956 © Helen Brack, reproduced with the kind permission of Helen Brack and the National Gallery of Victoria. 'Apology to John Brack' © John Spooner, 2010; Film poster, 'Bridge to Terabithia', 2007; Additional images from Shutterstock.